"Thanks to electronic technology, bullying has grown even more common in teen culture. And yet many parents remain in the dark in regard to the dangers lurking in cyberspace as well as the locker room. Nicole O'Dell not only shines a bright light on this dirty little secret, but she offers some useful hands-on advice as well. A great tool for anyone who cares about teenagers!"

—Melody Carlson, award-winning author of
Diary of a Teenage Girl and *TrueColors*

"Nicole O'Dell has created something that is—in my opinion—revolutionary in helping parents of teens. The idea of creating scenarios prior to issues arising and then coming alongside our teens to help them navigate those scenarios is going to help me a ton! My only regret is that I didn't read this book sooner. If you are a parent, pick this book up. It will make you think differently about how you communicate with your kids."

— Marybeth Whalen, Proverbs 31 Ministries writer and speaker, author of *The Mailbox* and *She Makes It Look Easy*

T0339013

Hot Buttons Series

Hot Buttons Internet Edition
Hot Buttons Dating Edition
Hot Buttons Drug Edition
Hot Buttons Sexuality Edition
Hot Buttons Bullying Edition
Hot Buttons Image Edition

HOT BUTTONS

BULLYING EDITION

Nicole O'Dell

Kregel
Publications

Hot Buttons Bullying Edition
Copyright © 2013 by Nicole O'Dell

Published by Kregel Publications, a division of Kregel, Inc., P.O. Box 2607, Grand Rapids, MI 49501.

The author and publisher are not engaged in rendering medical or psychological services, and this book is not intended as a guide to diagnose or treat medical or psychological problems. If medical, psychological, or other expert assistance is required, please seek the services of your own physician or certified counselor.

ISBN 978-0-8254-4243-8

Printed in the United States of America

13 14 15 16 17 / 5 4 3 2 1

The Hot Buttons series, as a whole, is dedicated to my mom who had to deal with more hot buttons when I was a teen than she'd care to remember. Also to my six children who have so graciously provided the research I needed to write these books . . . whether I wanted them to or not. And to my husband, Wil, who somehow managed to make my teen years look like a walk in the park.

Hot Buttons Bullying Edition *is for the kids who are afraid to go to school. May the Lord of peace comfort them and keep them safe against the enemies who come against them. And may they see themselves through His kind and loving eyes.*

➤➤➤ *"One's dignity may be assaulted, vandalized, cruelly mocked, but it can never be taken away unless it is surrendered."*

—Dr. Martin Luther King Jr.

Contents

Preface. 9
Acknowledgments 13

Part One: Bullying Hot Buttons
Chapter 1: Prepared: Answering *Why* 16
Chapter 2: Watchful: Answering *When* 26
Chapter 3: Proactive: Answering *How* 34

Part Two: Identifying the Bullying Hot Buttons
Chapter 4: The Victim. 46
Chapter 5: Cliques and Groups 56
Chapter 6: Cyberbullying. 65
Chapter 7: Self-Harm and Bullycide. 75
Chapter 8: The Bully 87

Part Three: Pressing the Bullying Hot Buttons
Chapter 9: Protective Procedures. 96
Chapter 10: The Armor of God 104
Chapter 11: Strategic Scenarios 112

Part Four: Parent-Teen Study Guide

Chapter 12: Confession 147
Chapter 13: Forgiveness 152
Chapter 14: Clean Slate 157

Recommended Resources 165
Notes. 167
About the Author. 169

Preface

Bullying.

Now if that isn't a societal buzzword, I don't know what is. We're worried about our kids being bullied, and we're even a bit nervous they'll act like a bully in the pursuit of popularity or to avoid abuse directed toward them. We're concerned they'll stand up to bullies and get the heat turned on them, but on the other hand, we're afraid they won't stand up to bullies and they'll be victimized.

It's exhausting to even think about the issue, let alone do something about it. And if we are ready and willing to act, what's the right thing to do? What advice do we give our kids? Fight back? Turn the other cheek? Tell a teacher?

I was bullied. Many of you were too, I'm sure. Those circumstances changed my life and have shaped who I am and what I think about myself. That story will unfold throughout this book and *Hot Buttons Image Edition*, because bullying and self-image often go hand in hand.

When it comes to our kids, it's less about teaching them to defend themselves, and more about teaching them to value themselves. We need to worry less about how they handle individual incidents and more about the despair or inadequacy they may be feeling.

As I've shared in each Hot Buttons book, the game of Scenarios came about years ago when I was searching for ways to lead my children to make good decisions. Knowing that young people learn best through personal experience, but also knowing that I didn't want to leave them on their own until they were faced with temptation, I decided it would be far better to talk to them proactively about issues they would one day face than it would be to wait until they were buried under the consequences of their poor choices.

I knew I'd have to be willing to talk about the tough subjects like sex, drugs, alcohol, addictions, dating, and pornography, perhaps even before they knew what those things were. If I had any hope of being as proactive as I wanted to be, no subject could be off-limits and nothing could be ignored.

The practice of working through Strategic Scenarios became a favorite activity in my home and proved invaluable in preparing my teens to make good choices. The best part was the talks we'd have after the choices were made and the consequences were presented. My children felt free to explore, ask questions, safely experiment with the options—and then, when similar scenarios came up in real life, they were prepared to make the right choices.

The topic of bullying is a bit different, though. It isn't necessarily a choice (unless we're talking about the bully's behavior), but it can definitely lead to a host of poor choices and identity issues. For that reason, I recommend that you read this book along with the support of *Hot Buttons Image Edition*.

The Hot Buttons series was birthed as a way for you, Mom and Dad, to bring the principles and practices of my family's Scenarios game into your home, and I trust you'll see the same results I have. Purposeful dialogue about hot-button issues gives you the opportunity to sneak in some "personal experience" while also teaching your teens and preteens that their opinions are important, and their confusion is valid. *Hot Buttons Bullying Edition* is a manual for those tough, preemptive discussions you need to have with your children about relationships and the proper treatment of others.

In general, there are five aspects to successfully battling worldly issues in our kids' lives:
- Time
- Communication
- Example
- Consistency
- Prayer

You'll find those five elements woven throughout every section of this book. In part 1, I cover the why, when, and how of confronting the issues preemptively and what to watch out for along the way. Part 2 looks at the specifics of what your tweens and teens face as it pertains to bullying.

In part 3, you'll be able to take away practical and precise words in the form of Strategic Scenarios that will help you press the hot buttons that relate to bullying. Scenarios cover issues like popularity, cyberbullying, texting, religious persecution, and disabilities and other perceived weaknesses. I'll share truths about the topic, help you figure out how to handle it in your own home, and give you a prayer you can pray to ask God to help you with that particular issue.

If you're familiar with Hot Buttons books, you've likely worked through part 4 already, where you and your children are walked through the dual processes of confession and forgiveness, both within your family and in your relationship with God, and have identified specific hot-button issues, worked to reverse mistakes, and worked to repair damage that may have already been done. I recommend that you work through the parent-teen study guide, even if you've done it before. The Lord will show you new things as you approach His Word for answers on each new hot-buttons issue.

Acknowledgments

Thanks go to Kregel Publications for taking on this Hot Buttons project and for allowing me the opportunity to tackle the issue of bullying. It's been a true privilege to work with the Kregel team. I especially want to acknowledge the efforts of my fearless editor, Dawn Anderson. Thank you for tirelessly working to shape these books into quality resources.

I also want to thank my Facebook and Twitter followers. You are always so great to fire back your personal stories and helpful input whenever I have a question. You'll see that your responses helped shape the direction of parts of this book.

As always, I must thank my family who are a never-ending source of support and encouragement as I labor over my writing projects. Whenever the content gets heavy or the doubts press in, you shine the light at the end of the tunnel and talk me through it.

And, most importantly, to my Savior, Jesus Christ, thank You for Your unconditional love that speaks to hurting and abused souls stuck in the mire of insecurity and bullying.

PART ONE

Bullying
HOT
BUTTONS

What exactly is a hot-button issue? A *hot button* is any issue that is likely to trigger intense reaction. It's a topic that people generally agree is inflammatory or controversial. It hits hard and is often confusing—usually life-changing—and so it *requires* attention from parents raising tweens and teens. My goal in writing these Hot Buttons books is to face these topics now, together, so you can walk your kids through the necessary prep work, rather than ignore the issues and wait until they creep up sometime down the road. You have the parental right and the godly responsibility to hit these issues hard, head-on, preemptively instead of simply reacting to the challenge-of-the-day. Once your teenager brings a subject up to you or you find out it's a problem, you've missed the opportunity to lay the foundation on that topic. Someone else already did it for you.

Prepared:
Answering *Why*

Since bullying is something that happens to your kids, not really something about which they have to make a moral decision, it might seem logical to just wait and see what happens. Why launch into a whole bully-education campaign if it's unneeded?

Here's why:

- ◀ Bullying can happen at any time.
- ◀ Early bullying may pass unnoticed by adults.
- ◀ The first response is the most important one.
- ◀ The experience of being bullied can affect many areas of life and spill over into choices and temptations.
- ◀ Your tween or teen might be tempted to act as a bully at some point.
- ◀ Your tween or teen is highly likely to witness bullying at some point.

This is another one of those issues that must be tackled openly and honestly before it actually arises in the life of your kids (or if it already has, hit it hard now). When I dealt with bullies for the first time, it came as a complete shock, out of nowhere, and I was not prepared to handle it. You'll see in later chapters, and in *Hot Buttons Image Edition*, how that bullying led me to make bad choices.

Merriam-Webster defines a bully as someone who is habitually cruel to others who are weaker.[1] Though bullies exist in all walks of life and at all ages and success levels, for the scope of this book we'll be looking at bullying that affects school-aged children from late elementary school through high school.

Bullying is pervasive. In fact, the National Education Association estimates:

Each weekday, 160,000 students skip school to avoid being bullied.[2]

A Clemson University study released in 2010, in which researchers surveyed 524,054 students at 1,593 schools across the nation to assess bullying in grades three through twelve, found:

Seventeen percent of kids reported being bullied two to three times a month or more. And many reported that it had been going on for more than a year.[3]

Aggressive. Antagonistic. Cruel. Those are some of the words that come to mind when thinking about bullying. Bullying is repetitive, or has the potential to be. It involves a power struggle over popularity, physical strength, or any other fear or desire that can be used as a means to control another person. More than just physical intimidation, bullying can include sexual innuendo, gossip, exclusion, and more.

Bullying takes various forms: *verbal*, *social*, and *physical*.[4]

Verbal bullying is saying or writing mean things, either privately, in front of others, or online (which has its own term—*cyberbullying*), and can involve

- Teasing or name-calling
- Sexual innuendos or comments
- Taunting—trying to goad someone into doing or saying something
- Threats—physical or otherwise

Social bullying will feed off the victim's desire for friends or popularity, and can threaten damage to the victim's reputation or relationships. Social bullying can involve

- Exclusion from groups or activities
- The spread of rumors, gossip
- Public embarrassment
- Social threats

Physical bullying involves real or perceived threats or actions against the victim's body or possessions. Physical bullying can involve

- Outright fighting
- Hitting, kicking, pinching, or other forms of physical abuse

　Prepared: Answering *Why*

- Spitting
- Covert tripping or pushing
- Stealing, hiding, or breaking someone's possessions

We're moms and dads, so the thought of our children suffering abuse like this at the hands (or mouths) of their peers is sickening. And equally disturbing is the thought that our own preteen or teen may be the one who behaves as the bully. We must do something to help rid our society of the drive and the attitudes that lead to bullying.

Dispel the myth of effective insulation.

As Christian parents, we try to insulate our families from negative outside influences, but bullying is one area where that's nearly impossible. It takes only one twenty-minute recess to turn our kid's world upside down. And all sorts of triggers can precipitate that kind of conflict. A look, a rivalry, the wrong shoes, even an unfounded rumor. So, if you don't take the time, ahead of the first conflict, to equip your son or daughter with appropriate knowledge and responses, a lot of damage may be done before you even find out there is a problem.

I'm sure you wish, as I do, you could walk with your kids through the battles of life—guarding and guiding them through each pressure-filled moment, each decision between right and wrong, each temptation. If only we could pray a bubble of protection around them, and not let them see or experience any of the grim effects of sin or poor choices—their own or others'. Or maybe we could simply horrify our kids with our own stories and impact their choices by sharing our experiences. We'd share what we learned, and they'd commit to avoiding those pitfalls and mistakes. Simple, right?

Unfortunately, that's just not the way it works.

Assuming your kids will be able to effectively navigate relationships and deal with bullies without preparing them to do so is like pushing them off a cliff and hoping they'll learn to fly before they hit the ground. Without the prep work to strengthen them and arm them with the tools they need they'll fall flat in the face of tough interpersonal conflicts.

Intentionally prepare.

Each pressure-filled moment of bully-induced fear or each temptation-ridden moment when a child considers mistreating another in the pursuit of popularity or approval is backed up with some level of preparation—the groundwork we've done, whatever that may be. In that moment, that foundation is the only resource our children have to turn to. In that instant, their commitment to right or wrong is what it is, and there's no opportunity for us to further gird it up in any way. They're on their own, with whatever tools we've already given them.

That might sound harsh or overstated, but it is reality. It's difficult to raise wise, godly young people who are willing to deny themselves the approval of friends, attainment of popularity, or a better social status. That commitment is birthed in our kids through training and an understanding of the big picture. Knowing that, do you want to work even harder to arm them with battle preparation?

Picture your tween at that first moment of experiencing the words of a bully. What will those words do? Will they bounce off the armor that's in place because of the preparation that's been done, or will they pierce right into the heart and mind, doing instant damage?

Take the mystery out!

Parents can help their kids achieve the level of advanced preparation they'll need to stand by

- helping them figure out why they should care;
- giving them the tools they need to succeed; and
- walking them step-by-step through the process of making good choices.

Why should they care? When your child is not the victim, what's in it for him to stand in the face of peer pressure or bullying, risking friendships, popularity, relationships? What about when your child is the victim, and she's being bullied into doing something she knows is wrong or even bullied about her relationship with God? Kids need to see the value in preserving their integrity in the face of bullying or other abuse.

Worse yet, what if your child is the bully? When we realize that our kids have mistreated another (and it's common even among Christian kids), we have a lot of work to do. There's often an emotional disconnect that prevents the bully from feeling compassion, and it's difficult to elicit a regretful or sorrowful response. We may need to eradicate an entitlement attitude in order to make the bully aware of the problems and to help them toward a balanced acceptance of self and appreciation of others.

What tools do they need? Our teens and preteens need options. A life busy with wholesome church activities and sports—rather than too much time home alone riddled with boredom and mischief with an Internet available for wreaking havoc on others or being bullied themselves. They need to be part of a family that is serving the Lord and they need to see parents who practice what they preach. They need to continuously grow in the knowledge of the Word and in relationship with God.

God-honoring parents must prepare kids for the backlash that inevitably comes from taking a stand against peer pressure and bullies. Persecution, disappointment, and even out-and-out rejection when they choose to stand for what's right should be expected.

Children need to reach their teen years already armed with the tools necessary to make the hard choices—willing to withstand and endure persecution for the sake of Christ. And they need to be prepared with the words and tools they need to keep themselves safe from bullies and to even use those incidents as a means of sharing God's love with others.

And they need . . . *you!*

How can they walk through this? They need you to walk them, hand in hand, step by step. Mom, Dad, guardian, youth worker—they need you to be aware of what's going on. They need you to know them well. Bullied tweens and teens are desperate for someone to notice what's happening to them. Much bullying could be avoided if Mom and Dad were highly involved at the start. This requires time, communication, and godly insight into the minds of your kids.

Prepared: Answering *Why*

We can be confident parents, even in these scary times!

Our kids are bound to face relationship struggles they are ill-equipped to handle, and it's very difficult not to panic. We realize that our kids' decisions related to peer pressure and the pursuit of popularity will affect the rest of their lives. We're torn between the extremes of denial—just letting go and hoping that everything will work itself out in the end—and tyranny—locking them up for a few years and checking in at, oh, around age twenty-two. We doubt we're up to the task either way.

We do have a promise to cling to, though.

> **Being confident of this**, that he who began a good work in you will carry it on to completion **until the day of Christ Jesus**. (Phil. 1:6)

Let's break that down.

Being confident of this:
You can be sure that this is the way it is. It's a promise.

He who began:
Who began it? "He" did. Not you. Not your teen. God started . . .

A good work:
The work He started is a good and righteous thing.

Will carry it on to completion:
It will be finished. He didn't start something only to see it fall to pieces because of some teenage mistakes. It will be completed. It's a promise of God, and I choose to believe Him.

Until the day of Christ Jesus:
Here's the thing, though. Every one of us, including our teens, is a work in progress. This work, which will be completed, has a long way to go . . . until the day of Christ Jesus, to be exact.

The battle we fight in protecting, shielding, and preparing our teens for life's hot-button issues isn't as black-and-white as a physical battle in which the wins and losses can be easily quantified. Bullying, popularity, and the choices involved are often internal matters of the heart that we may struggle to identify.

We must often blindly face the battles for our kids, operating more on faith than on sight, being obedient to the call of Christ and reliant on the leading of the Holy Spirit. We have been given tools in God's Word to prepare us to guard against the confusion of this world, however. And we're granted partnership with the Holy Spirit, who will lead and guide us according to godly wisdom and sight. That guidance is invaluable as we prepare our kids for the interpersonal conflicts they will face.

CHECK POINTS ▶▶▶

CHECK POINTS

✓ The experience of being bullied can affect many areas of life and spill over into choices and temptations.

✓ Bullying is repetitive, or has the potential to be. It involves a power struggle over popularity, physical strength, or any other fear or desire that can be used as a means to control another person.

✓ Bullying takes various forms: *verbal*, *social*, and *physical*.

✓ We must do something to help rid our society of the drive and the attitudes that lead to bullying.

✓ Each pressure-filled moment of bully-induced fear or each temptation-ridden moment when a child considers mistreating another in the pursuit of popularity or approval is backed up with some level of preparation, whatever tools we've already given them.

✓ Bullied tweens and teens are desperate for someone to notice what's happening to them. Much bullying could be avoided if Mom and Dad were highly involved at the start. This requires time, communication, and godly insight into the minds of your kids.

✓ We must often blindly face the battles for our kids, operating more on faith than on sight, being obedient to the call of Christ and reliant on the leading of the Holy Spirit.

Watchful:
Answering *When*

Bullying is nothing new.

It's been twenty-five years since I was bullied. And I have friends older than me who suffered much worse than I did when they were young. The power struggle of the strong versus the weak has been taking place since the beginning of time. Sadly, it's human nature.

Where times have changed is in the delivery. Years ago, students got shoved into lockers or had their milk money stolen. These days, they become victims of a cyberbullying campaign or a texting war. Instead of being embarrassed just among their classmates, they may be embarrassed on Facebook, in front of everyone they know. Where a few decades ago, bullying might have meant name-calling or skirmishes in the school yard, now it can include death threats and lead to suicide. The stage is larger and the stakes are higher.

The early years are for training our children. In Mark 14:38, we're warned to watch and pray about temptation. The spirit might be willing to avoid it, but the body is weak. How much more so for someone who isn't prepared for the temptation! We may have raised the most well-intentioned kids on the planet. But even though their spirit is willing, their flesh is weak—they need to be trained.

> Therefore you shall **lay up these words of mine in your heart and in your soul**, and bind them as a sign on your hand, and they shall be as frontlets between your eyes. You shall **teach them to your children**, speaking of them when you sit in your house, when you walk by the way, when you lie down, and when you rise up. (Deut. 11:18–19 NKJV)

The answer to *when* is *now*, and *routinely*.

The reason most teens today aren't influenced by Mom and Dad's opinion about new friends is because parents no longer exercise their right to have a voice or use their veto power in relationships. Many parents have forgotten that they have the right to deny access, to say no to friendships, to keep their teen home, and to do anything else that might keep their kids safe. Instead, many just roll their eyes at rudeness and disrespect, shake their heads at droopy pants and skimpy dresses, and turn a blind eye to the at-any-expense pursuit of popularity.

Many moms and dads have laid down their right to actually parent, and we can only hope and pray their teens will come to their senses before it's too late. So, rather than falling victim of the tragedy described above, take charge in your home. *When? Now. And always.*

What don't your kids want you to know?

Your kids don't want you to know how important being accepted is to them. They don't understand the drive that compels them to seek approval from others, and they certainly don't want you to know how far they'll go to make sure it happens. Your teenagers are embarrassed to have so high an opinion of others and so low an opinion of themselves. They also don't want to admit they're mentally exploring ideas and possibilities, and they want to conceal the things they're discovering about themselves and others.

You're not likely to hear about those first flirts with peer pressure. Your daughter is not going to come home and tell you that she bullied a younger kid that day, hoping to make herself look tough. Your son won't readily admit that he was teased mercilessly about his pimples, and spent the rest of lunch hiding out in the bathroom.

If you wait until you do discover these things, the effects will have already begun to take hold on their hearts and minds. Their lifestyle will have already begun to take a different shape and their relationships and reputation will have been affected either positively or negatively by being bullied or by being a bully.

So, knowing that they don't want to share these inner truths with Mom and Dad, it's important that you get intentional about this subject now. Before it's too late.

How early is too early?

I'm going to go out on a limb with this and say that this topic is a from-birth topic. By that I mean, this isn't some shocking topic that will rock their world when you bring it up for the first time. This one really goes back to the basics of treating others as you would like to be treated. Then, as the stakes get higher as your kids age, you can add more to the conversations.

If your daughter is going to chase hard after popularity in sixth grade, she needs to learn about the effects of bullying and peer pressure, and develop a plan for saying no, when she's much younger. Similarly, if she's going to be pressured to have sex in ninth grade, teach her how to say no in seventh. If your son's friends are going to be weight training and pressured to use steroids at seventeen, teach your son how to respect himself and his health far earlier than that. Assuming your teens will make it through those issues and temptations unscathed without preparation is naive. The same is true for navigating relationships.

You have to be willing to tackle tough issues openly and honestly before they actually come up. It might seem like informing them of the facts about bullying will plant unnecessary fear in their young minds or that they might think you suspect them of being mean to others. But you'll see, through the course of this and all of the Hot Buttons books, why there's really no such thing as "too early" when it comes to preparing your kids for temptation by arming them with truth. In fact, you'll see why earlier is far better than later.

Let me ask you some questions:

- Does your child show any interest in popularity?
- Has your child anguished over not having a boyfriend or girlfriend?
- Have you seen an upswing in the desire for trendy clothes?
- Have you seen any signs of friend shifting and rejection toward or from your child?
- Has your child expressed any dissatisfaction with his or her appearance, abilities, or character traits?
- Have any of your child's friends shown one or more of these tendencies?

If you answered yes to any of those questions, even the last one, the comparing game has already begun. It may already be too late for the kind of preemptive action I'm talking about, and you'll have to take more of a reactive approach—which is equally necessary. Don't misunderstand; I'm not saying that the topics addressed in the list of questions above are necessarily bad, but they are open doors that expose your kids to issues you need to address.

Let's go a step further. Consider these questions:

- Has your child recently changed BFFs?
- Has your teen withdrawn from activities or shown other personality changes?
- Are your kids ever home alone on the Internet?
- Have you noticed your tween's money or possessions missing? Or unexplained bruises?

Did you say yes to any of those questions? If so, you need to seriously consider that your child may already be suffering because of a bully, and seek the help of school staff and other professionals who can help protect your child. We'll talk more about that later in the book.

It takes time.

When it comes to popularity, self-esteem, and bullying, tweens and teens often believe adults are simply out of touch. That belief makes it difficult to respect the advice Mom or Dad offers. When I asked how their parents feel about popularity and bullying, these are some of the responses I received from teens:

> "They just don't get it. My mom says to be glad I'm not popular. That it's too much responsibility. Is she kidding?"

> "Just because Dad wasn't popular, that doesn't mean I can't be. It's like he wants me to suffer like he did."

> "Popularity is the only way to make it through my high school. I'll do anything to be popular. Mom just doesn't get that."

> "When I told my mom I'm being bullied, she brushed me off and said, 'There's too much in the media about bullying. It's just putting ideas into your head.'"

> "My dad says I should throw the first punch, or at least fight back. What if I don't want to?"

> "I know my parents love me. I just wish they'd take me more seriously when I tell them what's happening to me."

Ouch.

Before you're going to be able to make an impact regarding the hot-button issues, particularly regarding friendship, popularity, and bullying, you're going to need to gain trust. Your kids cannot ever feel that you're bored by or, worse, uninterested in, their concerns. If your teens think you just want them to go away, they will. If you are too busy to languish over this subject with your tweens, you're sending a message that it's really not all that important, and neither are they.

It might seem like training our kids who to watch out for and what to watch out for is doing the opposite of what we intend. It might seem like we're pointing out people's differences instead of minimizing them. The point is, we're not trying to *deny* differences, but *accept* them.

If my child didn't notice that a classmate was missing an arm, I'd need to have her eyes examined. But if we can acknowledge that missing arm and the natural difficulties that poses for that classmate, then I can guide her to respond with compassion, helpfulness, and acceptance.

So *when* do you begin teaching about bullying? *Now.* Take every opportunity to talk your tween or teen through appropriate, compassionate, godly responses to people who are different from them. Encourage them to observe the world around them.

CHECK POINTS ➤➤➤

Watchful: Answering *When*

CHECK POINTS

✓ Where a few decades ago, bullying might have meant name-calling or skirmishes in the school yard, now it can include death threats and lead to suicide. The stage is larger and the stakes are higher.

✓ The reason most teens today aren't influenced by Mom and Dad's opinion about new friends is because parents no longer exercise their right to have a voice or use their veto power in relationships.

✓ Many moms and dads have laid down their right to actually parent, and we can only hope and pray their teens will come to their senses before it's too late. So, rather than falling victim to that tragedy, take charge in your home. *When? Now. And always.*

✓ Your kids don't want you to know how important being accepted is to them. They don't understand the drive that compels them to seek approval from others, and they certainly don't want you to know how far they'll go to make sure it happens.

✓ The point is, we're not trying to *deny* differences, but *accept* them.

✓ Take every opportunity to talk your tween or teen through appropriate, compassionate, godly responses to people who are different from them. Encourage them to observe the world around them.

Proactive:
Answering *How*

The Bible teaches that we are to treat others as we wish to be treated. But social expectations, especially in middle school and high school, often dictate that kids push others down (literally and figuratively) so they, themselves, can rise to the top.

We talk to our kids about rules and choices. Maybe through the other Hot Buttons books you've even become convinced that it's necessary to bring up certain issues to your kids before they arise. But how do we develop a basic empathy toward others? How do we prevent bullying by raising kids who care more about the feelings of others than they do about their own? And when it comes to bullying, which happens every single day, how do we raise kids who can rise above it? And is it possible to do all of that through simple conversation?

Every Christian parent would agree that the ideal is for their teens and preteens to be nice to everyone and to have lots of friends. But, realistically, that isn't always the way things work out. Not everyone is popular. Not everyone gets invited to parties. Not everyone dates the captain of the football team or the head cheerleader. Are we willing to keep our eyes open and have ongoing dialogue with our kids starting as early as possible? If so, then we will have the opportunity to prepare our children to face all kinds of struggles, including bullies, with confidence and faith in God firmly in place.

I assure you, it can be done. Conversation, specifically Strategic Scenarios as you'll see later in this book, is one of the tools at your fingertips. But there are other necessary components, too. The best way to encourage open communication is with information and awareness. It's vital that you're educated about what your kids are dealing with, armed with the tools to guide them, and then ready to stand watch.

Whatever you do, don't *relate*.

Studies have shown that teens feel the most distance from parents who try to be their friends, contemporaries, buddies. They have peers at school, and most of their struggles revolve around those peers. At home, they need and want a parent.

This applies heavily to the issue of bullying, because bullying is firmly intertwined with self-esteem and the quest for popularity. Trust me, in their eyes, you sharing about your struggles over popularity and bullying is about as relatable as *The Brady Bunch*. Instead of trying to relate and be accepted by your teen as a contemporary, gain credibility by admitting and embracing your differences. Let your kids educate *you* about *today's* challenges. It will get them talking, and you'll learn something!

Your teens don't want you to feign interest in the details of their school day; they want you to guide them toward safety. They certainly don't want you to ignore what's happening here while they embark on the dangerous, peer-pressure-driven pursuit of popularity; they want you to set boundaries and teach them the way to walk. They don't want you to look the other way while bullies prey on them; they want you to be a lighthouse in the storm that leads them to the shores of safety.

What Not to Say
"I can relate."
"When I was your age . . . "
"Oh, this will pass."
"Wait until you have adult problems . . . "

Also avoid:
> Trendy speech
> Assuring them that someone else has it worse, or other seeming brush-offs.
> Trying to convince your son or daughter that this will go away—it's present now, that's all that matters.
> Belittling the issue—it doesn't feel like a small problem.
> Laughing—this hardly needs commentary, but it happens so often. Don't tease your teens about the things they worry about or the things bullies say.

What to Say
It's very important that you validate your teenager's thoughts, fears, doubts, and insecurities. Let them know that they are worthy concerns. We'll get into specifics on the issues of bullying in later chapters, but for now here are some key validating phrases that can go a long way toward bridging the gap between you and your teen:

"Wow. I can see why this would be a confusing situation for you."

"Ouch. That must hurt."

"Would you like advice, or do you want me to just listen?"

"It must be so frustrating to feel like they don't know the real you."

Whatever you do, don't be unapproachable.

In order to see a breakthrough on this issue, it's going to require a lot of conversation and the trust that will allow your words to sink in. One of the biggest problems that leads to mistrust and ineffective communication in the family is the lack of time. In fact, when asked what they don't like about adults, the biggest complaint teenagers had was that parents don't really take the time to listen. Below are some actual responses I received when asking teens that very question:

> "They pretend to hear by grunting, nodding, even sort of laughing when they think they should, but offer no real response to show me they even heard what I said."

> "They don't ask any questions about what I said. They're too happy I stopped talking and are afraid to 'put another quarter in' [a phrase that parent actually uses]."

> "Dad gets mad when I'm confused and just wants to spout out advice and expects me to take it without any further discussion."

"They're 'too busy.'"

"They say things like, 'Give me ten more minutes.' 'Not now, okay?' They aren't exactly rude, but they kind of brush me off."

"I know my mom loves me, but I just wish I could have a little face time for real."

Again, ouch!

Especially when you're covering the issues that go along with insecurity, if you are too busy to linger over this subject with your teens, if you're sending a message that it's really not all that important, and neither are they, even more damage can be done. More important than dealing with any specific issue or solving an immediate problem is the bigger point of letting your teen know you care enough to listen. Anytime. To anything. The feeling of rejection that comes when parents brush off concerns builds to a general resentment that leads to rebellion and anger.

Whatever you do, don't preach.

Once you've heard your teen's concerns, don't preach. No matter how much you study or how passionate you become about the nuggets of truth you uncover in the Word, if you don't hand it down to your teens in love, it's meaningless. Scripture should never be used to attack, browbeat, or belittle. You should never, ever use Scripture to make your teen feel bad about individuality.

Proactive: Answering *How*

Teens can tell if you've really taken the Scriptures to heart and applied them to your own life, or if you're just trying to do your spiritual duty by passing the doctrine on to them. They can tell if you're preaching out of control and fear, or if you're reaching out to them out of love and concern.

Instead, speak truth with love and respect.

I've learned the hard way over the years that knowledge spewed without love just sounds hollow. I've turned off many hurting people in my well-meaning attempts to reach them with God's Word. It's true, so they must want to hear it, right? Not always. At least not always right away, in that way.

> **If I speak in the tongues of men or of angels**, but do not have love, I am only a resounding gong or a clanging cymbal. If I have the gift of prophecy **and can fathom all mysteries** and all knowledge, and if I have a faith that can move mountains, **but do not have love, I am nothing**. (1 Cor. 13:1–2)

The knowledge of the *content* of the Bible without a grasp on the intent—the love—and without giving it the proper *context*, will never reach our teens. It cannot simply be a rule book. It's far too easy to rebel against rules. It must be a love letter.

Instead, be a model.

It's so important that we, the parents, are consistent on the issues ourselves. If we speak of treating others as Jesus would, but then model exclusivity in our own relationships, or if we speak of kindness and generosity toward those who suffer with weaknesses or disadvantages, but we show through our own actions that we have no time for those people, what kind of message are we really sending? We have to be 100 percent on these things, unwavering, immovable. When we are living as an example, it's far easier to call our kids to higher living, either in how they treat others or in how they feel about the way others treat them.

How hard are you willing to fight for your children's safety and well-being? Words and intentions are great, but do your actions as a parent support what you're asking of your kids? I have to look myself over and take stock of my answers to that question on a regular basis. Even the best of intentions can get muddied when they're in a tug-of-war with the world.

Here's the tough part, Mom and Dad. To be successful in raising teens, we need to spend more time modeling generosity and compassion toward others than we do making sure we fit in and have approval ourselves. Do you live in such a way that you are above reproach on this issue? How can we ask our teenagers, who are far less prepared to deal with life's temptations than we are, to make good decisions if we're not modeling the difficult behaviors in front of them? How can we expect them to overlook our shortcomings and choose better for themselves? When things get tough, you'd better believe they'll use our failures as excuses to justify their own.

To have the best life for your teen, you need to be living the righteous life yourself. In 1 Corinthians 9, Paul writes to the church about just this topic. He warns against preaching the truth to others but living in such a way that you miss it yourself:

> Therefore **I do not run like someone running aimlessly**; I do not fight like a boxer beating the air. No, I strike a blow to my body and make it my slave **so that after I have preached to others, I myself will not be disqualified for the prize**. (vv. 26–27)

Be honest about your struggles and temptations—let your teens know it isn't simple for you to win the fight against peer pressure and to treat all others as Jesus would. Be open about the cost of doing the right thing so they'll know they're on the right path. Give them insight into your teen years and the things you faced. But be honest. If you pretend you are someone you aren't, you might tip the scales in the wrong direction as your teen is unable to relate to you and your supposed choices. It helps when teenagers can see their parents as human beings with weaknesses, failures, and struggles. They don't feel so alone in the battle.

Instead, provide real-life practice.

Don't be afraid to let your teenager try and fail at interpersonal relationships. It's okay that it's happening as long as you're aware and using each exposure or challenge as a learning opportunity. But even better than letting them learn their lessons the hard way—with real-life people and their real-life pain—utilize the Strategic Scenarios provided in this book. If you work through them with your preteens and teens, you'll be providing the real-life practice they desperately need without sacrificing their own or someone else's feelings.

Combat the lies with the truth.

Your teen is feeling insecure, what are some of the ways she is unique and valuable?

Your teen is feeling uncool, what is the truth about his interesting qualities?

Your teen is feeling unattractive, what makes her beautiful inside and out?

Your teen is feeling unworthy, what does God say about the worth He finds in His children?

It's no secret that we all battle insecurity and doubt from time to time. But it's our job as parents to combat the lies the enemy throws at our teens with the truth of God's Word. What does God say about our teenagers?

Remember, we aren't fighting against people—against bullies. We're fighting against Satan who longs to keep our teenagers embroiled in self-doubt and personal struggles. Bullies are one of the ways he comes against our kids.

We're at war!

Not with our kids . . . for them.

> For **our struggle is not against flesh and blood**, but against the rulers, against the authorities, against the powers of this dark world and **against the spiritual forces of evil** in the heavenly realms. (Eph. 6:12)

CHECK POINTS ➤➤➤

Proactive: Answering *How*

CHECK POINTS

✓ The Bible teaches that we are to treat others as we wish to be treated. But social expectations, especially in middle school and high school, often dictate that kids push others down (literally and figuratively) so they, themselves, can rise to the top.

✓ Teens and tweens don't want you to look the other way while bullies prey on them; they want you to be a lighthouse in the storm that leads them to the shores of safety.

✓ If we speak of treating others as Jesus would, but then model exclusivity in our own relationships, what kind of message are we really sending?

✓ Words and intentions are great, but do your actions as a parent support what you're asking of your kids?

✓ Be honest about your struggles and temptations—let your teens know it isn't simple for you to win the fight against peer pressure and to treat all others as Jesus would. Be open about the cost of doing the right thing so they'll know they're on the right path.

✓ Even better than letting them learn their lessons the hard way—with real-life people and their real-life pain—utilize the Strategic Scenarios in this book, which provide real-life practice without sacrificing their own or someone else's feelings.

PART TWO

Identifying the Bullying HOT BUTTONS

Although the vast majority of us at least witnessed bullying, if not experienced it firsthand, and maybe even participated in it, most of us have an unspoken expectation that we'll be able to protect our kids from bullies. Somehow we think our kids are immune to the sinful choices and struggles that we faced. That kind of wishful thinking, with eyes closed to the truth, is unhealthy for us. And potentially dangerous for our kids.

An understanding of right and wrong and the resolve to always do the right thing have to be taught, not just absorbed. We need to identify the bullying hot buttons so that we'll be aware of the risks our kids face, and can prepare them for the tough choices and pressures that inevitably await.

4 The Victim

There are certain perceived weaknesses in those who are bullied. I say "perceived weaknesses" because it's actually a myth that the weak are bullied by the strong. In fact, it's the bullies who are weak—emotionally and sometimes physically too. They lash out at others in an attempt to make themselves appear stronger or more important than those they bully. It's their own insecurity that convinces them that by making others look small and weak, they will look big and strong.

Younger bullies often come from dysfunctional homes, and are usually psychologically immature. They try to compensate for their lack of strength, control, or self-worth by bullying others and often learn that technique at home. By the time kids reach middle school, bullying occurs for a variety of reasons, but more commonly in misguided efforts to achieve social advancement. Those behaviors can happen regardless of the home environment.

Kids who are targeted by bullies are usually
> nonviolent,
> respectful of others,

- intelligent,
- and often verbal;
- and they almost always have a strong sense of fairness.

Yes, there are times when bullies target students with special needs or disabilities, but you'll find that those students too fit a good number of the traits listed above and perhaps that is part of the reason they are targeted. Bullies are driven by jealousy and envy and have an obsessive compulsion to torment anyone whom they see as better than they are, or whose success and happiness may only serve to reveal the bully's flaws.

Hopefully you've already read *Hot Buttons Image Edition* and have explored your responsibilities as a parent in steering your kids through the self-esteem and body image issues that often go along with being bullied or even being a bully. That book is really a companion to this one as it addresses many of the foundational mental and emotional patterns that can lead to being bullied or even to being a bully.

In looking at perceived weaknesses and how they can lead to bullying, we need to zero in on several issues. We'll take a brief look at them here, but *Image Edition* goes into much more detail.

Body Image/Appearance

Allow me to share a bit of my story with you. The summer before I entered middle school, I went to Bible camp where I got bit by a mosquito, from which I contracted encephalitis. That mosquito changed my life. I learned new words like *thyroid* and *hypothalamus*. I'll skip the gruesome medical stuff and get right to the end result: it messed me up. I gained a lot of weight in a very short amount of time and started junior high nearly twice the person I was when the summer started. Literally.

On the first day of junior high, I knew I was in for it. Entering that school was like walking up to a hangman's noose. Dread increased with each step.

At first, nothing happened. Then I found out why: most of the kids didn't even recognize me. Until my name was called during attendance. First I heard a few snickers, and then a boy I'd known my whole life called me *Butterball*. In front of everyone.

The ensuing months were horrifying. I was bullied in every sense of the word and hated trying to get through the school day. This went on through all of middle school, and there was nothing I could do about it. I was one of the lucky ones, though: I had a couple of good friends who stuck beside me, and I was involved in my youth group at church, so I wasn't home, bored, and lonely like many in my situation might have been. But I was hurting.

But things change very fast in the life of a teenager.

The summer before I entered high school, I went through puberty with a vengeance, and the hormonal shift threw my body back into working order, at least to a degree. I went on a major diet and added in a ton of exercise . . . and I started high school at an average weight.

On the first day of high school, the boy who called me *Butterball* hit on me.

In that moment I tucked away an internal expectation and acceptance that appearance was what mattered.

Appearance. Body size. Wardrobe. Skin type. Those are some of the things that cause tweens and teens angst as they seek the approval of their peers. Clamoring to become worthy or popular (whether or not the demands are real, implied, or just assumed) our kids are pressured to become something they often are not.

Many times they are physically unable. A tall, large-boned girl cannot force herself into an award-winning gymnastics career or, often, a cheerleader's uniform. A small boy with a bent toward the sciences isn't going to become captain of the football team no matter how hard he tries. It's often the frustration of trying to fit into shoes that simply do not fit that creates a desperation that can lead to being bullied.

Teach your kids:
- ➤ You are beautiful in God's sight because He created you just the way you are.
- ➤ Sacrificing self-respect for the approval of others is not worth it.
- ➤ There's no winner in the battle for perfect appearance—it's better to rise above it by not competing in it.
- ➤ Bullies are weak and feel insecure about themselves—don't submit yourself for their approval.

Popularity, or the Lack Thereof

The instant that boy started flirting with me on the first day of high school, I learned that looks were all that mattered, and if I wanted to get people's attention, I'd better capitalize on them. So I did. In the ensuing months, as I had the opportunity to rise to a new level of popularity, I took every chance I had. I wasn't going to allow myself to ever again feel like I'd felt during middle school.

When I dressed in the perfect clothes, did well on the swim team, got my hair cut the way the popular girls wore theirs, said yes to peer pressure, and alienated my old friends . . . guess what . . . I was popular. It worked!

But there was a cost.

That pursuit of popularity cost me the respect and trust of my parents. I lost the BFF I'd had since first grade—the one who'd stuck by me through those tough middle school years.

My grades fell along with my self-respect.

Eventually, it cost me my virginity as I was date raped, and then followed that with one bad choice after another.

Popularity is a state of mind, and it's up to each individual to decide not to grant that kind of power to others, whether as a result of intentional peer pressure and bullying or not. Why let someone else decide one's worth? Why submit to someone else's arbitrary standards?

Help your tweens and teens rise above the pursuit of popularity that will swallow their soul. Encourage godly friendships and enlist the aid of a good mentor who has walked the same path.

At-Risk Groups

There are some groups of kids who are at greater risk of bullying simply because of their connection with certain societal groups.

Special needs or disabilities. This is a perfect example of the cowardice of bullies. They choose to pick on the perceived weaknesses of a person with special needs and torment that individual, believing he or she can't fight back or won't get angry. Parents, teach your tweens and teens to watch out for people with special needs and be ready to defend them.

Race or ethnicity. When bullying based on race is severe it can be labeled *harassment*, which is covered under federal civil rights laws. Teachers and administrators need to be on guard against this cancer that spreads. Parents, teach your kids to view each person as an individual, equally loved by God.

Religion and faith. In my research, I found that bullies don't tend to target religions per se, but they do target religious practices. Carrying a Bible or other religious book, wearing long skirts or head wraps, celebrating religious holidays, praying, abstaining from certain foods or activities—all are things that bullies don't understand and perceive as weakness. Parents, teach your kids to respect religious practices, even those you don't observe yourself and may even disagree with.

Sexuality. Kids who identify as gay or lesbian, or who portray cross-gender traits, are definitely at an increased risk of being bullied. In fact, according to recent studies, "adolescents who report same-sex romantic attractions or relationships are at more than 2 times the risk for suicide attempts,"[5] and "it has been suggested that victimization may be a leading factor in the high rates of suicidality that have been demonstrated in past studies of gay and lesbian youths."[6] No matter what one's beliefs about homosexuality are, these kids need to be protected. (See *Hot Buttons Sexuality Edition* for more information on teen homosexuality.)

Have a quirky kid?

My brother used to carry sardines in his lunch box. He'd put that little key in the top and the other kids would look on in interest as they bit into their PB&Js. He'd turn the key so the top would roll back, exposing those oily little suckers and allowing their odor to waft across the table.

"Ewwww!" Kids would grab their brown bags and snatch their Twinkies as they slid as far away as they could get, noses wrinkled in disgust.

Bryan would pick up his plastic fork and dig in as though he didn't even notice their reactions. Maybe he didn't, or maybe he didn't care. Either way, he was hungry.

That quirky kid also asked for caviar and smoked salmon in his Christmas stocking, and once took apart his handheld game devices, rewired them, and made a Morse code machine that hooked up to a transistor radio—which he also made from parts.

Quirky. Smart. Unique.

I give my mom a lot of credit for not trying to convince him to leave the kippers at home for an after-school snack. She let him be himself without making him feel like a zoo exhibit.

You might have a child who acts differently than others his age. Or your daughter might be creative but ahead of her time. In a youth culture that demands conformity, how do you ensure that your quirky kid is happy and well-adjusted? How do you deal with all of the perceived weaknesses mentioned and multiple others not listed here?

Recommendations:
> Encourage growth by exposing your child to new things.
> Ensure acceptance from siblings—don't allow siblings to exert anger or bully by other means like disgust, rejection, embarrassment, belittling, and disapproval.

- ➤ Communicate your complete love and acceptance for this child. Leave no doubt, in his or her mind or anyone else's.
- ➤ Confirm your child likes him- or herself.
- ➤ Find someone—friend, role model, youth worker—with whom your child can specifically relate.
- ➤ Involve the school in watching out for red flags like sadness, isolation, or potential bullying.
- ➤ Intervene when necessary.
- ➤ Keep an open door to opportunity and allow your child to try new things and discover new interests.

Another caution I want to offer: Be very careful not to send a message that you're concerned a perceived weakness or quirky or unique behavior might result in bullying. This validates the perceptions of the bully; affirming that it is okay, right even, for bullies to pick on people who don't fit the mold. For example, never say something like, "Do you want them to pick on you?" or "You're wearing that? You're just begging to get beat up." You get the idea. Bullying is abuse, and it's never the fault of the victim. Don't send the message to your wonderfully unique child that any abuse she suffers is her own fault.

If you feel the need to address certain behaviors and preferences, do that separately, not at all in response to any bullying or angst related to outside influences. Wait until a time when you can have a conversation that has nothing to do with other people, when you can say things like: "Are you sure that's the way you want to handle that?" Or, "Would that be better left for home? Maybe that could be our special thing."

Celebrate your unique child as a human being and, in a world that cries for conformity, embrace his or her qualities as a gift. Don't let the light go out on the sense of self that allows your son or daughter to enjoy free self-expression. This doesn't mean you have to allow hair dye, tattoos, piercings, or gang membership. It just asks you to embrace your beautiful, unique child for the person God created him to be.

Lord, I love my child so much it hurts my heart to think that others don't celebrate those special things that warm my heart to its core. Please help me gird my child with self-confidence, help me love the way You do, and help me deal with hurts that come because of mean people—bullies. Please protect my kids from dangers and emotional pain that can happen during these tough years of middle school and high school. And please make me aware of what I need to see, even if my child doesn't tell me what's going on. Amen.

CHECK POINTS ➤➤➤

The Victim

CHECK POINTS

✓ Bullies lash out at others in an attempt to make themselves appear stronger or more important than those they bully. It's their own insecurity that convinces them that by making others look small and weak, they will look big and strong.

✓ It's often the frustration of trying to fit into shoes that simply do not fit that creates a desperation that can lead to being bullied.

✓ Parents, teach your tweens and teens to watch out for people with special needs and be ready to defend them.

✓ Bullies don't tend to target religions per se, but they do target religious practices.

✓ Ensure acceptance from siblings—don't allow siblings to exert anger or bully by other means like disgust, rejection, embarrassment, belittling, and disapproval.

✓ Be very careful not to send a message that you're concerned that a perceived weakness or quirky or unique behavior might result in bullying.

✓ Celebrate your unique child as a human being and, in a world that cries for conformity, embrace his or her qualities as a gift. Don't let the light go out on the sense of self that allows your son or daughter to enjoy free self-expression.

Cliques
and Groups

From preschool to high school graduation, kids just want to fit in. Close friends offer a sense of validation. The very presence of a BFF is tantamount to approval. It's like saying, "Hey, you're alright. You matter. I like you." Having layers of relationships from the close BFF to teammates to acquaintances is important, but tweens and teens spend an inordinate amount of time worrying about their social status.

Friends vs. Cliques

It is very natural for tweens and teens to group together according to style, interests, location, and other criteria. In fact, it's a good thing when like-minded people can spend time together because it's validating and it encourages personal growth. As circumstances and shared interests bring students together regularly over a period of time, friendships develop naturally. A healthy group of friends, even when they are the most popular kids at school, embraces individuality and accepts flaws. It doesn't require certain dress or speech, and it definitely doesn't demand the shunning or bullying of others.

A *clique* can be defined simply as a group of friends that is exclusive. That sense of closed-door membership inherent to a clique is not true for a natural group of friends. But it's the exclusivity that often makes inclusion with a clique even more desirable and important. If not everyone can get in, it's more special for the ones who do.

Clique members often protect the exclusivity of the group by being mean to those who try to infiltrate. Sometimes it goes even further to where someone outside the group is targeted or victimized. Instead of being centered on shared values or interests like a healthy group of friends, cliques tend to focus, even subconsciously, on maintaining a certain social status. Where true friends stick around for the long haul, clique members are at constant risk of being dropped if loyalty is questioned or social status falls.

"And parents buy into it," says Rosalind Wiseman, author of *Queen Bees and Wannabees*. "Mom and Dad remember what it felt like when they weren't allowed to buy the clothes and shoes that the popular kids wore. Now they feel like they're failing kids if they don't get them the hottest jeans. But they're not."[7] When parents engage in the scramble to fit in, they're sending a message that they believe their kids need help in order to be liked or have friends. It's the wrong impression to give kids. We want them to celebrate themselves, not their wardrobes. We want them to feel confident in their individual contribution to the group, not become a clone. What kind of sense of self-worth will that message inspire?

Why do cliques bully?

Bullying is a way for clique members to feel better about themselves and to reinforce the power they've claimed and the exclusivity of the group. Many tweens and teens believe they will gain more popularity if they make fun of others and spread gossip because it will ingratiate them to some group or another—they may not even realize that's bullying, but it definitely can be.

Robert Faris and Diane Felmlee studied 3,722 middle and high school students over three-plus school years and found that the teenagers' levels of aggression rose commensurate with their social status. Aggressive behavior peaked when students hit the 98th percentile for popularity, suggesting that they were working hard to claw their way to the very top. "Individuals at the bottom of the status hierarchy do not have as much capacity for aggression," says the study, "while those at the very top do not have as much cause to use it. But for the vast majority of adolescents, increases in status are, over time, accompanied by increases in aggression toward their peers."[8] Bullying is an issue of power. It's a stepping-stone to achieving power over someone.

Cliques bully others in order to:
- ➤ Get attention. Power-hungry teens thrive on being noticed.
- ➤ Get what they want. Often, bullied kids become "slaves" to the bully.
- ➤ Be respected. If other kids see them as "in charge," they are revered.
- ➤ Climb the popularity ladder. They have to prove allegiance to the clique.
- ➤ Improve self-esteem. A bully appears bigger (in his own eyes) by making others appear small.
- ➤ Get back at others. Bullied kids bully kids.

> Get pleasure from inflicting pain on others. Depression and other mental concerns caused by bullying or abuse can lead to problems like this.
> Follow the leader. The best way to stay in a clique is to act just like its members.

While we may not understand the logic behind bullying behaviors, the fact that they've been going on for generations proves the validity of the issue. It's real. It happens. And most tweens and teens who seek popularity find themselves on the dishing end of bullying behaviors at some point. Understanding why it happens is important for prevention.

There is a social-status hierarchy in schools. We all know it exists, and that very structure is fodder for much bullying and angst as students struggle to climb that ladder and get pushed down by the higher-ups. Each child handles this differently and places a different level of importance on his or her position in that structure. For example, one of my teenage daughters really doesn't care. She wants to be friends with whomever she chooses and doesn't wish to be in the "most popular" group because there's too much pressure and, as she perceives it, it's too fake.

She's stylish—but in a very different way than her peers. She's confident, but more mature than many of her classmates. She's managed to rise above the structure. Yet, at times I see hints of peer-group hierarchy creep into decisions she makes and things she says, even though she's unaware of it.

My other daughter is much more focused on popularity. She ranks the groups in her school by levels: level 1, level 2, level 3, etc. Statements like these frequently fly around my home:

"Well, she's in the number three popularity group and the other girl is a number one. It'll never work out."

Or

"I was a three, but now that I'm friends with her, I'm more like a two. I probably don't ever want to be a one, at least not if it means I can't still be friends with my BFFs who are fours."

And to my question about how many levels there are:

"At least six, but it could be seven. It just depends."

Alrighty then.

How about you and me?

We spend a lot of time talking to our kids about including everyone, treating people as Jesus would, not focusing on popularity, and so on. But I wonder: What kind of models are we? Now, stick with me. I'm speaking to myself as much as to you. We're all friends here, right?

What kind of message are we sending to our kids? Maybe we go to a Bible study or to coffee with our closest friends each week. How easy would it be for a newcomer to show up at one of those groups? And if a newcomer were accepted, would he or she look just like all of us? How readily would we accept someone new from a completely different walk of life?

We can't expect our kids to handle the desire for popularity or to fight the peer pressure to classify people into categories of worth if we are unable to model the behavior we expect from them.

Whether in the school yard, or in the church pew, social ranking exists. The question is, how do we respond to it? Who do you talk to around the church? Whom do you seek out for coffee, committees, and friendship? Worship leaders may be looked up to as much as the captain of the football team. You may seek out attention from a small-group leader just like our kids revere the jocks and cheerleaders. It's easy to congregate around attractive people, to compliment and affirm them. But what about the reclusive, despondent, or sullen? Or the aggressive, loud, or angry? What do your kids hear you say about them? How do they see you interact among those people groups?

Ultimately, people are people, but as a society we are divided into groups in every possible way. Socially, financially, emotionally, and physically; clubs, affiliations, teams, and denominations. Yes, it's natural to spend the bulk of your time with people who share interests and do similar things, but what about the missionary heart of a Christian? Are we modeling it to our kids?

We need to live as Christ among the diverse groups in our church and neighborhood, and then to the world. We can't sit back and wait for the needy to come to us. It's up to us to go to them.

> Therefore **go and make disciples** of all nations, baptizing them **in the name of the Father** and of **the Son** and of **the Holy Spirit**. (Matt. 28:19)

Have a cliquey kid?

Whether your child is on the inside looking out or the outside looking in, cliques can cause confusion and longing. Help your child look into those important relationships and evaluate what they promote. Do they actually share interests and values? Do things go on that have to be overlooked, like bad decisions, peer pressure, or dishonesty? Do those friendships hurt or benefit your child's reputation? And, ultimately, does your tween or teen feel good about those friendships?

Recommendations:

1. Continue to talk it out.

Ask lots of questions about the social hierarchy at your child's school. Find out who's who, what's expected, who sits where at lunch, and anything else that might be important. Expect to have many conversations about this and use the information to steer your kids to wisdom.

2. Don't lose your cool.

Things may not be going well for your child at school, but remember, sometimes they learn best from some small mistakes. Give plenty of time for your son or daughter to work through the issues with your guidance, but save the mandates for when they're absolutely necessary. Of course, if there are physical threats or other sorts of bullying happening, it's necessary to jump in and work with teachers to formulate a plan.

3. Regularly offer a way out.

Sometimes tweens and teens stick with a clique or a group of friends because they can't figure out how to get out. By making suggestions, offering new activities, supporting new requests like joining a team or participating in a new sport, you might be providing a necessary way out of a damaging clique.

Father, I lift up my teens to You right now. Please place a hedge of protection around them and help them stay focused on the prize—the end prize, not the goal of popularity or inclusion in a clique. Help them withstand peer pressure and say no to all forms of bullying. Help me guide my teens to have a long-term perspective that understands goals and consequences rather than a short-term view that seeks worldly satisfaction. Show me what I need to see, and give me the right questions to ask so I can respond to situations immediately. Thank You for loving them so much. Amen.

CHECK POINTS ▸▸▸

CHECK POINTS

✓ A healthy group of friends, even when they are the most popular kids at school, embraces individuality and accepts flaws.

✓ We want our kids to celebrate themselves, not their wardrobe. We want them to feel confident in their individual contribution to the group, not become a clone.

✓ Most tweens and teens who seek popularity find themselves on the dishing end of bullying behaviors at some point.

✓ We can't expect our kids to handle the desire for popularity or to fight the peer pressure to classify people into categories of worth if we are unable to model the behavior we expect from them.

✓ Whether in the school yard, or in the church pew, social ranking exists. . . . We need to live as Christ among the diverse groups in our church and neighborhood, and then to the world.

✓ Whether your child is on the inside looking out or the outside looking in, cliques can cause confusion and longing. Help your child look into those important relationships and evaluate what they promote.

✓ Give plenty of time for your son or daughter to work through the issues with your guidance, but save the mandates for when they're absolutely necessary.

chapter 6

Cyberbullying

An individual tormented or in some way targeted by a bully in an online setting or even via text message has become so pervasive that, in 2000, a new word was coined: cyberbullying. Cyberbullying involves the use of devices such as computers, tablets, smart phones, and gaming systems, and occurs in chat rooms, via text message, and through social media sites. It can be direct, where the bully communicates directly with the victim, or indirect, where the bully posts rumors, photos, accusations, fake social media profiles, or anything else about the victim.

Some stats you should know:
> - Forty-three percent of teens have been victims of cyberbullying in the past year.
> - Nearly 80 percent said they did not have parental rules about Internet use or found ways around the rules.
> - Only 11 percent talked to their parents about what they'd experienced.
> - Ninety-two percent of teens who were cyberbullied knew their victimizers—half of those teens knew the cyberbullies from school.[9]

Cyberbullying is usually one component of, or an extension of, a bully-victim relationship that already exists in person, usually at school. It's often not the only form of bullying a child experiences and, in that way, serves to exacerbate an already overwhelming situation.

Kids who are cyberbullied have a harder time getting away from the behavior. That might seem counterintuitive because, well, if you're being bullied online, just go offline. Right? But, these kids tend to be afraid to log off or avoid the Internet because they know the bully is still at work, posting comments or pictures, and they want to be aware of what's being spread around about them. It's difficult for them to walk away. Like being unable to look away from a horrifying accident scene.

What makes cyberbullying different?

Cyberbullying can be particularly vicious because of its potential for anonymity. Bullies are cowards, so it's natural that they'd get tougher when hiding behind a computer screen. Many say they think it's funny to torment others online because no one can do anything about it. Since they don't have to face their victims, they don't have to justify or even recognize the pain they're causing. When friends goad them into doing more, it only takes the push of a few buttons to ramp up their campaign against the victim. Cyberbullies feel secure in believing they won't get caught. They can see the effectiveness of their bullying without the consequences.

And, many times, that sense of anonymity and safety offers enough assurance that people who would ordinarily never get involved in face-to-face bullying do jump in on cyberbullying scenarios. They might take the opportunity to try it out and see how it makes them feel. Then, since they can't really see and identify with the effects it has on the victim, or at least not right away, it continues over a longer period of time than it might have if it happened in the school yard, in plain view of everyone.

For the victim, knowing that cyberbullying can happen 24/7, at any moment of the day or night, can have a maddening effect. They don't need to be on guard just during school hours, but at every moment. It can cause fear, loss of sleep, depression, and more. Since an attack can be spread through the Internet anonymously, the victim may not even know its source with 100 percent certainty, which compounds the fear and insecurity he or she feels.

And, we mustn't forget, words and pictures posted to the Internet are permanent. It's very different than threats made in a school yard or verbal insults slung across a classroom. Even hand-scribbled notes can be discarded, never to be seen again. But the effects of cyberbullying are far-reaching and virtually impossible to erase, potentially following the victim for years.

Furthermore, schools are not equipped or empowered to help stop cyberbullying. If the acts take place off school grounds and outside of school hours, the school's proverbial hands are tied. If they take action against a student's behavior outside of school, they can, and often are, sued for various violations of their authority and the student's right to free speech. And they often lose.

What the school *can* do:

> Teach students the law on cyber activity, including the consequences. Many don't realize that possessing or even opening pictures or emails in some cases can be illegal.

> Communicate with the parents when a cyberbullying situation arises. Work with them to stop the problem.

> Add a clause to the school's policy that gives the right to hold students accountable for anything they do that endangers or affects the well-being of another student.

> Work with a legal team to defend authority for off-campus cyberbullying actions.

Effects of Cyberbullying

Cyberbullying has long-lasting effects on kids, and understandably so. Tweens and teens who are cyberbullied are more likely to:

- Face in-person bullying
- Use alcohol
- Use drugs
- Skip or resist school
- See a drop in grades
- Experience depression
- Battle low self-esteem or body image issues
- Practice self-harm or consider suicide (see chapter 7)

As with any form of mistreatment or abuse, when young people are cyberbullied, feelings of anger can cause the victim to lash out at the bully. They may retaliate in similar form or find another way to get revenge.

Preventing Cyberbullying

How can you possibly stop something as insidious as cyberbullying? Do you ban the Internet from your home? Well, you could, but then you'd also have to yank it out of the school and the library and all of your kids' friends' homes, too. Oh, and don't forget confiscating all the smartphones. No, the technology itself isn't to blame for cyberbullying, but cyberbullying is a clear risk when technology is employed, so steps must be taken to prevent it.

First of all, you should debunk the idea that there is anonymity on the Internet. That's simply not true. There's always a way to track someone down and follow their activities on the Internet. Even long after the fact.

You can also discuss the consequences of being a cyberbully. In many cases it violates the terms of use with Internet service providers or companies like Yahoo or Google, and they can close all accounts associated with any bullying. You should also mention the legal ramifications that can result even from online threats. For example, does your teen realize that bullying could lead to a police record?

Most important in the prevention of bullying is to purposefully remind tweens and teens that basic respect for others also extends to online behavior. If teens would remember that there are real people, with real feelings, behind that computer screen, perhaps they'd have a harder time causing the trouble they do. Pray for them and with them, that they'd have compassion for others and not let the violence in this world desensitize them to other people's hurts.

Hot Buttons Internet Edition can help you establish safe boundaries for your kids regarding Internet use, including:

- Talking with tweens and teens about the dangers lurking on the Internet.
- Exposing the potential for inappropriate things that could happen online.
- Following your teens' online activity and checking up on them in the places they frequent.
- Communicating rules about Internet use, setting measurable guidelines and concrete consequences, and then consistently upholding those rules.
- Keeping computers in a main area of the home.

Make a response plan.

Your tweens and teens need to be educated on what to do not only if they are cyberbullied, but also if they are tempted or pressured to cyberbully someone else, or if they feel the urge to retaliate against a bully. It's easy for even the most well-meaning kids to get so sucked into the clamor for approval that they resort to mistreating others. Cyberbullying is a sort of gateway into that behavior because of its apparent anonymity and impunity. Open communication will be your primary tool.

Recommendations:

> Make it safe for your child to come to you with problems and concerns. Don't be quick to answer or judge. Listen, pray, and avoid responding in the emotion of the moment.

> Guide your kids in how they will respond when faced with someone who is bullying either them or someone else. Using the Strategic Scenarios will help start those *what if* conversations.

> Guide your kids in how they will respond to the temptation to bully others. Help them accept themselves, and help them accept others.

Too late for prevention?

Maybe you've recently discovered that your child is being cyberbullied. It's too late for prevention. What now?

As you prepare to handle this dilemma, remember that you're the lighthouse, the beacon in the storm. Parents should be the safe zone, a trusted place where kids can turn for protection, encouragement, and validation. Remembering that will help you offer an appropriate response to your child's reports of bullying. It's important that you don't overreact with broad, sweeping moves like unplugging the computer, calling parents, calling the school, and so on. But it's also important that you take swift and confident action, showing your child that you're in control.

Step one. Call the school guidance office and let them know what's been going on so they can watch for signs of any trouble at school—face-to-face confrontations, but also academic problems, behavioral changes, mood changes.

Step two. Get into your computer and print out any evidence you can find of the bullying. Also take screen shots and make sure they're dated. You may have to trace your child's traffic through the browser history, check email accounts, visit Facebook pages, and so on. Delete nothing. (Parents: It's possible that during this search, you'll find that your teen has been involved in some inappropriate activity too—inappropriate conversations in chat rooms, or whatever it might be—but now is not the time to deal with that. Validate your daughter's right not to be bullied; guarantee your son your protection *first*. After that situation is resolved, go back and deal with other hot-button issues that have arisen.)

Step three. If there is any sign of physical threats, contact the police immediately.

Step four. Ask the police or volunteers at WiredSafety.org about how to ask your Internet service provider not to delete the online evidence. Servers are usually scheduled for routine emptying and it's easier to retrieve information before that happens.

Step five. Decide if it's wise to reach out to the bully's parents. Sometimes it is; sometimes it isn't. If you have a personal relationship with the parents, then I recommend that you do reach out. They need to know what's going on. Sometimes, though, since we know bullies bully others, there's a chance there are problems in that family. If you aren't sure, it would be better to talk to a guidance counselor at the school and either ask for advice, or ask that she or he reach out to the family if appropriate. This would be true for all kinds of bullying.

Step six. Seek professional help if needed. There are often things about which your child won't feel comfortable being completely honest with you. An unbiased, professional third party like a counselor, therapist, or pastor is a great way to make sure your son or daughter gets the necessary help.

Guarding your tweens and teens against cyberbullying before it happens is the best approach, and being open and consistent in your communication about it is the best way to achieve that goal.

It's so scary, Lord. I love my kids so much, and I just want to shield them from all the craziness out there, but at some point I know I have to let go of the fear, entrust them to You, and believe that they'll be okay. Please protect them from bullies and from all dangers that lurk online. Give me wisdom to know what's okay and where I should put limitations. Please help me to see what I need to see and then respond in effective ways. Amen.

CHECK POINTS ▶▶▶

CHECK POINTS

✓ Cyberbullying is when a person is tormented or in some way targeted by a bully in an online setting or even via text message.

✓ Forty-three percent of teens have been victims of cyberbullying in the past year. . . . Only 11 percent talked to their parents about what they'd experienced.[10]

✓ Cyberbullying is usually one component of, or an extension of, a bully-victim relationship that already exists in person, usually at school. It's often not the only form of bullying a child experiences and, in that way, serves to exacerbate an already overwhelming situation.

✓ Knowing that cyberbullying can happen at any moment of the day or night whether the victim is present or not can have a maddening effect. It can cause fear, loss of sleep, depression, and more.

✓ Parents should be the safe zone, a trusted place where kids can turn for protection, encouragement, and validation. Remembering that will help you offer an appropriate response to your child's reports of bullying.

✓ Guarding your tweens and teens against cyberbullying before it happens is the best approach, and being open and consistent in your communication about it is the best way to achieve that goal.

Self-Harm
and Bullycide

Victims of bullying are often initially targeted because they are seen as peaceable people who are unwilling to lash out in anger or harm others. When abuse happens, rage is inevitable, and so suppressed feelings of anger and the desire to retaliate pile up in these individuals and can cause depression or other health concerns. When victims are unable or unwilling to retaliate against the bully, they often focus their revenge onto their own bodies.

Self-harm can include many different means of damage to the body: excessive drinking, drug abuse, eating disorders, cutting, even attempted suicide. In any form, self-harm can have serious, long-lasting, even permanent effects on the body.

How do kids self-harm?

In a 2006 study of 2,800 college students, 17 percent reported having participated in self-harm and most of those claimed to use two to four methods of self-injury.[11] It's also important to note that many of the students surveyed had never been in therapy and most had never disclosed their self-injurious behavior to anyone. In other words, there were no treatments in place and the students hadn't already reached out for help.

Scratching or pinching. More than half of the respondents who admitted to self-injury claimed this as their method of choice. They admitted to scratching to the point of bleeding and pinching until bruises formed. Watch for fresh scratches and unexplained bruising on a regular basis.

Impact with objects. This involves hitting oneself with objects or punching things to the point of bruising or bleeding. Thirty-seven percent of respondents admitted to this behavior. Look for swelling in odd places accompanied by bruising. Typically, if a tween or teen is naturally injured badly enough that there is significant swelling or bruising, you'd have heard about it when it happened, right? So if you're seeing injuries that weren't mentioned at the time they occurred and the explanations don't add up, dig deeper.

Cutting. Just over 30 percent of those students who admitted to self-harm were involved in cutting and the majority of those were girls. Watch for rows of cuts at various stages of healing, often on the forearms, wrists, or stomach, and the propensity for wearing long sleeves or heavy clothing, rows of bracelets or wristbands.

Self-impact. This includes hitting oneself or activities such as jumping into walls. Twenty-five percent of the students who reported self-harming behaviors used this method. Again, watch for signs of unreported injuries or too frequent injuries. Don't allow your teen to brush this off as no big deal or just for fun.

Ripped skin. Ripping or tearing skin is a form of self-injury seen in 16 percent of the self-injurers. This is commonly done on the hands, sometimes absentmindedly. Watch for bleeding and raw spots along fingernails.

Carving. A step beyond cutting, carving is actually cutting words or symbols into the flesh. Around 15 percent of respondents had done this. Watch for letters or anything purposeful carved into the skin. The goal may be to scar, creating a sort of tattoo, but it can also be to send a message.

Impeding healing. This includes picking scabs or irritating wounds at various stages of healing. Watch for injuries that seem to drag on without getting any better. Of the 13.5 percent of respondents who did this, most did it in tandem with another form of self-injury.

Burning. Burning was seen in almost 13 percent of students who self-harmed. Watch for blisters, cigarette burns, burns in odd places like the forearms, or symmetrical blisters that might signal intentional burns.

Stabbing or shoving objects into the skin. Glass, needles, pins, razors, and other sharp objects are shoved into the skin. Pain is welcomed as a relief. Twelve percent of responding students used this method.

Pulling out hair. The uncontrollable urge to pull out their own hair was seen in 11 percent of students who self-harmed. Watch for thinning hair, bald spots, and clumps of hair in the bed or on clothing.

Eating disorders and addictive behaviors are not generally considered self-harm. An eating disorder may be triggered by the taunts of a bully who calls the victim fat, for instance, but then the motivation is to lose weight, rather than an attempt at self-harm. They can definitely be means of self-harm though, if the psychology behind the action is disgust with oneself or is driven by a subconscious desire to get back at the bully.

The same is true for tattoos and/or piercings. Those things can simply be a form of self-expression, but they can also be a cry for help or a form of self-harm.

It might seem like nothing but semantics to take the time to make that distinction, but it's very important to identify the cause of a behavior so you can find an effective treatment for it. A good counselor or therapist should be able to wade through the actions and the motivations to find the truth. You can also check out *Hot Buttons Image Edition* for more help with body image and self-esteem.

Why do they hurt themselves?

Children who are bullied are three times more likely than others to self-harm by the time they are twelve years old, according to a new study.[12] Twelve. That is so young. The reason it's such a problem for young people all the way through college is that they are dealing with things they can't control and often can't verbalize. They feel alone and ashamed. In that light, self-injury is not necessarily an attention-seeking tactic, though many people assume that to be the case. Rather, it's often a way to deal with pain in silence, in an attempt to avoid further attention.

Also, we know that injuries (whether naturally occurring or self-inflicted) trigger a dopamine release from the brain as the body tries to cope with pain and begin to heal itself. Young students who are suffering seek solutions. This dopamine release and subsequent healing offers a natural relief as the body does its job. Subconsciously, it feels good to see the body suffer and heal.

Tweens and teens have expressed the following reasons for their self-injury:

- It allows them to hurt in a different way than the abuse.
- They can't express their feelings.
- It's a reminder that they aren't invisible.
- It's something they can control.
- The physical pain hides the emotional pain.
- They feel worthless.
- They hope someone will notice.
- They feel guilty about something.

Are kids who self-injure likely to commit suicide?

Most self-injury is non-suicidal. That's not to say that a tween or teen who does attempt suicide or commits suicide has never self-injured. It's just that studies have shown the motivations behind them are opposite.

It's possible, though, that self-injury might desensitize the person against pain or injury, making it easier to take further measures.

In a study put out by the American Medical Association, Dr. Janis Whitlock, states, "Since it is well established that SIB [self-injurious behavior] is not a suicidal gesture, many clinicians assume that suicide assessment is unnecessary. Our findings suggest that the presence of SIB should trigger suicide assessment."[13] The study goes on to show that even though they are not interlinked—that is, suicide is *not* necessarily the last step of the ladder of self-harm—the markers of both are commonly present in the same people.

> We hypothesize that while individual SIB acts are rarely, if ever, undertaken with suicidal intent, SIB signals an attempt to cope with psychological distress that may co-occur or lead to suicidal behaviors in individuals experiencing more duress than they can effectively mitigate. If so, suicidal behaviors would be likely to either co-exist or evolve over time if SIB begins to fail as a functional coping mechanism.[14]

Suicide, or bullycide as has been recently coined to refer to suicide in response to bullying, is generally chosen when escape seems to be the only option, the only way out of intolerable circumstances. It may be an attempt to punish the bully or make an indelible statement about how much pain the bully had inflicted. Or a suicide attempt may be a cry for help, with no real death wish attached.

While self-harm is usually not a gateway to suicide since they are for different purposes and seek to solve different problems (self-harm predominantly addresses the internal, personal, psychological trauma and suicide is more an attempt at escape or punishment), bullying can lead to both responses in the same or in different victims. In other words, just because someone self-harms, that doesn't indicate they are at risk of suicide. And just because someone is not engaged in self-harm behaviors, that doesn't mean they are not at risk of suicide.

Why don't kids ask for help?

Statistics from the 2008–2009 School Crime Supplement show that an adult was notified in only about one-third of bullying cases.[15] And one study found that "the older kids were, the less likely they were to talk to parents or teachers about . . . bullying."[16] Why is that? For one thing, kids don't believe that adults can protect them. "For example, 30 percent of boys in grades three through five said their teacher had done little or nothing to reduce bullying, as compared to almost 60 percent of boys in grades nine through twelve."[17] As parents, it's horrifying to imagine that our kids would be suffering and keep it completely to themselves, that they'd turn to self-harm before reaching out to a parent or teacher. How could that be?

There are actually many reasons bullied kids don't involve parents or other adults:

  ◀ Bullying often makes a child feel weak, inferior, and helpless. If they can handle it on their own, they feel a sense of empowerment and control.

- They don't want to get further ridiculed as a baby or tattletale.
- The fear of backlash can be crippling.
- Kids who are bullied often feel humiliated. They don't want to have to tell anyone what's being said about them or done to them.
- They sometimes fear being punished for weakness—and sometimes kids are "roughed up" for not being tough enough.
- Feeling isolated, they may begin to believe—or maybe already believed—what's being said about them.
- Many fear losing the support of the few friends they have left.
- They believe the adults in their life either don't care or won't have the power to stop the abuse or protect them from its effects.

This is why it's so important to keep the lines of communication open in the home. Make it easy for your children to confide in you. Be a refuge in the storm. As parents, we never want to be on the other side of tragedy looking back, wishing we had heard their cries for help, seen signs of their pain, or acted in some way that showed them we had their backs and would do whatever it took to keep them safe and secure.

But we're Christians!

How can Christian tweens and teens, raised in Christian homes, suffer so much hopelessness that they have to harm themselves to feel better? Parents I've spoken to over the months and years leading up to this book feel helpless and confused when it's discovered that their child is cutting or injuring his or her body in some way.

Sixteen-year-old Amber says it well:

> "We [Christians] have to be perfect. If we're bullied or hurt in some way, we're supposed to turn the other cheek and not fight back. We're supposed to always be an example to people. But sometimes it just hurts. When do we get to feel our pain? To cry?"

That mistaken perception that Christian teens have to be perfect is the impetus for self-harm because they simply want to feel and to be heard. Their bodies are crying out for justice, but their minds have no idea how to go about getting it. This is especially true in the case of bullying. The charge of a Christian to teach others about God and to love one's enemies is counterintuitive when there is bullying or abuse involved. That leads to confusion about what God expects and about the truth of the bullied person's individual value.

The solution to this, as with most things, is to address it head-on with your preteen or teenager, something like this:

Hey, I don't know if you're going through any bullying or if you're having trouble with friendships or anything else at school. I'm definitely here to talk about things like that if you want to. But I also want you to know that God suffers when you suffer. He doesn't want or expect you to be in pain and carry it alone. He wants you to have help from others and to feel His love so deeply. Here's what He says about you and your pain:

Therefore, it was necessary for him **to be made in every respect like us, his brothers and sisters**, so that he could be our merciful and faithful High Priest before God. Then he could offer a sacrifice that would take away the sins of the people. Since he himself has gone through suffering and testing, **he is able to help us when we are being tested**. (Heb. 2:17–18 NLT)

What can you do about it?

Breaking the cycle of self-harm is difficult because it's often involuntary or compelled by something the self-injurer doesn't understand, and is therefore difficult to control. Most times, the teenager wishes she or he could stop. When they do realize they're doing it, and make the conscious choice to engage in the behavior, it's because they're getting something psychological or physiological out of it that no amount of logic will overcome. In order to stop the cycle of self-injury, a person has to make the choice to do it, and make a commitment to that choice. It has to be voluntary and willful.

But, you, Mom and Dad, can be a catalyst for that commitment. There are several things you can do to begin the healing process and to point your kids in the right direction:

- Enlist the aid of a counselor or therapist, preferably a Christian one.
- Use call centers or online resources. (Check the recommended resources at the back of this book for suggestions.)

- Build a support structure for your teen. People like youth workers, pastors, aunts, uncles, mentors, teachers—people you and your teen can both trust and who have expressed care and concern for your child—are all good choices. If you have several kids, pick different people for each one, so they have a private place to go that's all their own.
- Help your kids help themselves. Provide alternatives for self-harm by offering outlets for frustrations, places for expression of creativity, access to friends, and so on. Other coping strategies can be found through the resources listed at the back of this book.

Ultimately, keep your eyes and ears open, and be flexible. What was true for the circumstances of today may not be true when things change tomorrow. What helped today may not have any effect tomorrow. Be willing to see the whole situation and respond accordingly. And, most importantly, be in constant prayer for the safety and well-being of your teen and for your own wisdom as a parent.

Father, thank You for Your promises. Thank You for loving my kids even more than I do. Please help me to be an extension of You in their lives. Show me what I need to see so I can parent them effectively. Keep them safe and hopeful in Your enduring promises. Crowd out any feelings of doubt or insecurity with abundant love and grace so they will see themselves the way I do . . . and the way You do. Please love them through me. Amen.

CHECK POINTS

✓ When victims are unable or unwilling to retaliate against the bully, they often focus their anger onto their own bodies.

✓ Self-harm can include many different means of damage to the body: excessive drinking, drug abuse, eating disorders, cutting, even attempted suicide. In any form, self-harm can have serious, long-lasting, even permanent effects on the body.

✓ Children who are bullied are three times more likely than others to self-harm by the time they are twelve years old.[18]

✓ There are many reasons bullied kids don't involve parents or other adults. . . . This is why it's so important to keep the lines of communication open. Make it easy for your child to confide in you.

✓ That mistaken perception that Christian teens have to be perfect is the impetus for self-harm because they simply want to feel and to be heard. Their bodies are crying out for justice and their minds have no idea how to go about getting it.

✓ In order to stop the cycle of self-injury, a person has to make the choice to do it, and make a commitment to that choice. It has to be voluntary and willful.

chapter 8

The Bully

It's Tuesday morning. You have your coffee cup in one hand and your Bible in the other. It's time for your weekly women's Bible study group—a favorite break from your normal weekday routine. You take your usual seat and small talk begins around the table. You've been going to Bible study with these women for years and most of you send your kids to the same Christian school.

It's prayer request time. One of the women asks for prayer for her daughter who is enduring horrendous bullying at that very Christian school. You're absolutely horrified to hear all that has been going on.

"Wow. I'm stunned. I've not heard stories about any of this sort of behavior from my girls. Not at all." You sip your coffee, grateful that your daughters have been spared.

The woman's eyes narrow. "Well, no, I guess you wouldn't have heard the stories, would you?"

You blink a few times. *What does she mean? Is she saying . . . ?*

So, what if this were you? What if you found out that your child had been bullying other children? Naturally, you're going to assume that it's all a mistake, a misunderstanding, a case of mistaken identity.

Denial, at its core, isn't a bad thing. Of course you want to give your kids the benefit of the doubt. And of course it will seem odd and even unlikely that you'd missed the signs all along. But, the evidence must be considered at face value, and the truth must be confronted.

Maybe you'll have trouble believing the reports. I know I would. But you can't deny eye-witness accounts from a teacher or other school staff member. Or, if a child's parents report things their child has said and it can be corroborated by other students or teachers, you'll need to take it seriously.

You'll likely move from denial to self-blame, and maybe some self-pity. *What have I done wrong as a parent? What's wrong with my kids? Why me?*

After you've accepted the truth as it is, you'll probably allow some anger to set in. Toward yourself, toward your child, toward the other parent who brought it to your attention. Both misplaced and valid emotions will mingle together. That's all normal. But, still, you have to act.

Or, maybe no one has said a word to you, but your parental instincts have kicked in and something just isn't right. There are some signs you can watch for to see if your tween or teen may be acting as a bully:

- Frequent name-calling—either in front of the victims or behind their backs
- Inflated ego
- Bragging
- Pushy and controlling behaviors
- Gravitates toward weaker kids
- Unsympathetic and lack of empathy
- Argumentative
- Defensive
- A loner
- Aloofness

The Bully

My child is a bully. What now?

Perhaps you've identified, either by someone pointing it out to you or by your own discovery, that your child is a bully. While most everyone has the potential for slipping into varying degrees of bullying behaviors in certain circumstances, there are two main types of bullies, and they happen to be polar opposites. One is the ultra-popular, socially powerful leader who influences others to bully as well. These people bully as an exertion of power and to prove status. The other kind of bully is the dark isolated individual who might seem depressed or angry. This type of bully often has low self-esteem and acts alone or in a small group. In order to address this effectively, you'll need to figure out where your child falls on the continuum.

Also, you're going to want to determine if the bullying is simply due to lashing out in response to being bullied. If it is, you'll want to address that immediately. Let your son or daughter see that your number one goal is to make things right for everyone. Don't show so much righteous anger about the bullying that occurred that it overshadows the pain your child has felt—if that's the case.

One challenge for bullies is that the problem circles back around and builds on itself. When a person acts as a bully, their status usually declines. This can often lead to increased bullying in efforts to regain or attain a higher level of popularity. That doesn't work . . . and so on. This is why it's vital to get some professional help for your tween or teen who has been bullying. It's not enough to just discipline them at home through grounding or removal of privileges. Whether it's the school counselor or someone outside the school, you need someone who is trained to address the underlying cause for the bullying.

Action Steps

Involve the school. You should get in touch with a teacher or the school guidance counselor right away. If they weren't the ones to alert you to the bullying, ask if they have seen any bullying behavior. They are with your son or daughter every day and should be able to give you more insight into what's been going on. Let them know that you are concerned and want the problem resolved. When they know you're a parent who will get involved and take steps to end the bullying, they will rally with you in a team approach.

Talk openly with your child. Have a heart-to-heart and lay everything out in the open. Let your son or daughter hear the words of the accusations being made and the response of the school. Share openly about the effects the bullying has had on the victim, specific quotes if possible, and ask direct questions like: "How does that make you feel?" "Was that the result you were hoping for?" "How would you feel in that same situation?"

Establish a safe period. As strange as this may sound, this isn't the time for punishments or anger. Your child needs help, not consequences—at least at this point. Once counseling is underway and the underlying causes are being addressed, then you can implement consequences directly related to specific behaviors.

Help make amends. One big fear of bullies is that they'll have to face their accuser and admit what they've been doing. Humility is not usually a strong suit for a bully. So, once you've explained the damage that's been done, help your child identify with the feelings the victim must have. Role play some ways to apologize and some steps to take to make it right.

Consider your own influence. What examples are you setting regarding the exclusivity of your relationships and the things you say about others? What are you allowing to occur between siblings? What sorts of entertainment are you allowing in the home? Do you participate in gossip or backstabbing? Sometimes a combination of factors desensitizes tweens and teens to the feelings of others, and causes them to elevate their own social needs above what's appropriate and acceptable. Be sure you're modeling grace and acceptance of others.

Bring it to the friends. Whenever you have an opening—a sleepover, a car ride, a dinner visit—talk to your child's friends about bullying and the effects it can have. If you discover that your child's friends are bullies, you need to step in and sever those relationships. Encourage activities that will help new friendships develop.

Most importantly, have realistic expectations about how this is going to go. Changes will come, but they won't happen overnight. Follow those steps listed above over and over until you see changes begin, and ask questions to help you keep tabs on your child's thought processes:

- How are things at school?
- How have kids responded to you as you've begun to change your behavior toward others?
- What's an example of a conflict you faced and how did you handle it?
- What has been the hardest part of making this change?
- How does it feel to know that others think of you as a bully right now?

This wouldn't be a Hot Buttons book if I didn't encourage you to be proactive. So, of course, the very best way to handle this situation is to prevent it in the first place. I know, that's often easier said than done, and sometimes that doesn't even seem like it would have been possible. But, you do have some important tools and a great opportunity to begin to chip away at this problem before it arises in your family.

You've taken a great first step by reading this book. Now, I encourage you to work through the remaining chapters, particularly the Strategic Scenarios, with your tweens and teens. If you take a stand against bullying now and have open conversations with your children, and if you prepare your kids in advance with good alternatives and a healthy self-esteem—neither underdeveloped nor overinflated—you're off to a fabulous start.

Father, thank You for allowing the Holy Spirit to speak truth into my family. Help me to keep an open watch on my children, always aware of changes and problems that need to be addressed. Let me not be blind to the needs my kids have or to the mistakes they make. If I need to recognize certain behaviors or poor choices in my teens, please help me to do it swiftly and then to act justly, according to Your Word. Please grant me the grace I need to be loving, but firm, and the ability to really affect a change in the situation. Thank You for loving my kids even more than I do. Please love them through me. Amen.

CHECK POINTS ▶▶▶

CHECK POINTS

✓ Your first goal is to determine if your child's bullying is simply due to lashing out in response to being bullied.

✓ When teachers and school officials know you're a parent who will get involved and take steps to end the bullying, they will rally with you in a team approach.

✓ This isn't the time for punishments or anger. Your child needs help, not consequences—at least at this point.

✓ What examples are you setting regarding the exclusivity of your relationships and the things you say about others? What are you allowing to occur between siblings? What sorts of entertainment are you allowing in the home?

✓ Have realistic expectations about how putting an end to your child's bullying is going to go. Changes will come, but they won't happen overnight.

✓ If you take a stand against bullying now and have open conversations with your children, and if you prepare your kids in advance with good alternatives and a healthy self-esteem— neither underdeveloped nor overinflated—you're off to a fabulous start.

PART THREE

Pressing the Bullying HOT BUTTONS

This is where the hard work comes in. You have the information you need; now you can put it into practice to really make a difference for your teens and your family. I encourage you to take every segment in the rest of this book very seriously—even if you've already seen something like it in other Hot Buttons books. The process may seem similar but the application for each issue is vital.

Since we're dealing with both victims and bullies, the focus will be a bit different for each family depending on the situation. That's okay—whether as prep work to avoid potential problems or in response to existing problems, the answer is the same. God's Word is true in all situations and the truths of confession, forgiveness, and grace are principles that apply to all of life.

Protective Procedures

The biggest piece to this puzzle is to build your child's self-esteem to a healthy place where confidence thrives and arrogance dies. At that place, your kids will feel secure in who they are, and will value others enough to empathize with them. If you haven't already, this is a great time to utilize the *Hot Buttons Image Edition*. The goal of that book is to help every tween and teen attain a healthy self-esteem.

But, regardless of self-esteem, everyone deserves to feel secure and physically safe, so when it comes to bullying, the worst thing to do is avoid the issue. If you think it doesn't apply because you've seen no signs of it, that's the ideal time to crack the issue open!

Who is at risk of being bullied?

You can read more in chapter 4 about the victims of bullying, but, sad to say, it's the kids who have something different about them, who stand out among the rest, who are not a carbon copy of the other students—those are the ones who generally suffer the work of bullies.

You can look for one or more of the following risk factors:
- ➤ Different in some way: glasses, braces, acne, overweight, underweight, poor, rich, smart, religious, etc.
- ➤ Under- or overdeveloped in some way: physically, emotionally, intellectually
- ➤ Unable to physically defend themselves
- ➤ Sad, morose, depressed
- ➤ Friendly and kind
- ➤ Honest and morally upright
- ➤ Desperate for approval
- ➤ Few friends to provide backup
- ➤ Spends a lot of time at home alone and online
- ➤ Attends a new school

That's not a comprehensive list, nor is it a guarantee that any combination of those things will lead to bullying. But if you're watching for risk factors, and you're aware of any telltale changes in your child's behavior, demeanor, or dress, you'll be in a good position to act swiftly should a bullying situation arise.

As discussed in chapter 4, victims of bullying are not at fault. Be careful not to zero in on traits your son or daughter might be exhibiting; don't assign blame there. If it seems to your child that you think a personal quality is the reason your child is being bullied, it will also seem as though you condone the abuse or at least understand why someone would want to be hurtful.

Signs of bullying

Not all children who are bullied exhibit warning signs, but there are definitely some red flags you can watch for that may signal a problem.

You can look for one or more of the following warning signs:
- Unexplainable or frequent injuries
- Missing possessions or money
- Feigned illnesses or undiagnosable injuries
- Excessive hunger after school
- Changes in eating habits
- Trouble sleeping
- Acts withdrawn, quiet, or passive
- Change in schoolwork or grades
- Reluctance to participate in social situations or accept invitations from peers
- Feelings of helplessness or decreased self-esteem
- Self-destructive behaviors, such as running away from home, self-harm, or talking about suicide
- Few friends
- No interest in activities previously enjoyed
- Mood changes—more fearful, sad, irritable, depressed, or angry

If you recognize any of those signs in your children, take notice. Some of those changes will be natural and normal, of course. As kids mature, their interests and friendships often shift. Adolescence can certainly bring mood swings unrelated to peer difficulties like bullying. Proactive discussion can help you learn the line in your child between normal and abnormal, between hormonal and hurting.

Along with the ongoing conversations and open communication you'll already be having about bullying, popularity, relationships, and peer pressure, as we've been talking about throughout this book, there are some other things you can do to address the problem.

Recommendations:

> Take your kids seriously. Show complete belief in and compassion for whatever they express to you. Be on guard against trying to defend the bully just to try to keep peace or in hopes that it isn't a serious problem.
> Build your kids' self-confidence by allowing plenty of opportunities to enjoy personal interests and develop skills. Be involved in and supportive of what they're doing.
> Build your kids' social skills. Provide opportunities for them to interact with peers and develop friendships. Help them become involved in group activities, such as sports, music, or art to improve their ability to make and keep friends.
> Use the Strategic Scenarios in chapter 11 in order to practice responses and open doors of communication.
> Practice specific responses. Encourage your kids to speak up for themselves, to say no to abuse, and to get help immediately from trusted adults without breaking down or letting the bully see emotions. Bullies thrive on eliciting an emotional response from victims, but, as we've already discussed, they are seldom able to respond

with sympathy, at least not without parental or professional help. It's important for victims to be honest about feelings, but primarily in trusted situations, like with parents or a counselor.

➤ Model compassion to all types of people. Set a good example by including people in your life, showing compassion to people who are different from you, and defending yourself in righteous ways.

Signs your child is bullying

Hopefully by now you realize that you should be on the lookout for bullying behaviors coming from your children. If you see some of the signs listed below, it doesn't mean you've been raising a hardcore bully, but it might mean that there's some confusion or social struggle at work. It's important that you tackle the issue and don't overlook the signs, because, left unchecked, this kind of behavior only escalates.

Watch for:
➤ Associations with new friends who have reputations for bullying
➤ Fighting in school
➤ Unexplained changes like more money and new possessions
➤ Anxiety over wearing just the right thing
➤ Blaming others for their problems
➤ Denial of problems when they're pointed out
➤ Rationalizing bad choices
➤ Increase in competitiveness
➤ Concern about reputation or popularity
➤ Enjoyment of violence—video games, books, weaponry

When it's your child who is bullying others, it's a hard thing to face. We never want to admit that our kids might be acting in a way that is harmful to others, but in order to help them develop good skills and find quality friendships, we need to help them break the cycle of bullying. The only way we can do that is if we first admit there's a problem.

You can help a child who bullies by:
> ➤ Working through the steps offered in chapter 8.
> ➤ Being loving. A kid who bullies is not a bad kid, just someone who needs to learn more positive ways of interacting with others.
> ➤ Talking about life. Find out what's going on. Some children bully when they feel sad, angry, lonely, or afraid and/or when there are major changes at home or school.
> ➤ Developing clear expectations and consequences. Set clear standards about what kinds of behaviors are acceptable and unacceptable. Let kids know what the consequences of bullying behaviors will be and apply consequences consistently.
> ➤ Intervening immediately. Take immediate action when you observe bullying; other children need to be kept safe and your child needs to know that you place that safety as paramount.
> ➤ Teaching good friendship. The secret to having good friends is to be a good friend.
> ➤ Modeling self-control and empathy. While impulsive, self-centered behaviors are normal in younger children, there should always be a conscious effort to correct those sins and train kids to be aware of the needs of others.

> ➤ Getting professional help. Since we've already shown that kids who bully were or are often bullied themselves, it's important to find out what's driving the behavior. Talk to a therapist, youth pastor, or guidance counselor.

Here are a few questions to ask yourself:

> ➤ Have I prayed over the topic of bullying before bringing it up to my teen?
> ➤ Am I taking biblical ideals and making them relevant issues for my kids?
> ➤ Am I using too many personal examples or lectures that my teens can't or don't want to relate to?
> ➤ Do my children feel free to ask questions? Am I prepared to give or find an answer if they do? Is there any subject that's taboo in my home?
> ➤ Am I offering application techniques, or just handing down rules?
> ➤ Am I offering practical alternatives to counteract boredom or hostility and to build a healthy self-image?

While the world laughs as we continue to abide by biblical standards, Christian parents must be willing to have uncomfortable conversations and make unpopular decisions in order to give our kids the best God has for them. As we saw in chapter 1, our kids need to believe that the Lord has a plan for them and that His ways are best. They need to be directed to fill their time in positive ways. And they need to know that their parents are watching out for them, always ready to listen.

CHECK POINTS ➤➤➤

CHECK POINTS

✓ Build your child's self-esteem to a healthy place where confidence thrives and arrogance dies. At that place, your kids will feel secure in who they are, and will value others enough to empathize with them.

✓ If you're watching for risk factors, and you're aware of any telltale changes in your child's behavior, demeanor, or dress, you'll be in a good position to act swiftly should a bullying situation arise.

✓ Encourage your kids to speak up for themselves, to say no to abuse, and to get help immediately from trusted adults without breaking down or letting the bully see emotions.

✓ If you see signs that your child may be bullying . . . it might mean that there's some confusion or social struggle at work. It's important that you tackle the issue and don't overlook the signs, because, left unchecked, this kind of behavior only escalates.

✓ We never want to admit that our kids might be acting in a way that is harmful to others, but in order to help them develop good skills and find quality friendships, we need to help them break the cycle of bullying. The only way we can do that is if we first admit there's a problem.

✓ While the world laughs as we continue to abide by biblical standards, Christian parents must be willing to have uncomfortable conversations and make unpopular decisions in order to give our kids the best God has for them.

The Armor
of God

In the Hot Buttons series, we talk a lot about the "armor of God" and how it helps in making good choices. The armor of God is vital when it comes to the risks to personal safety, self-esteem issues, and damaged relationships that can accompany bullying. Bullying can be both physically and emotionally damaging and its effects are long-lasting, often permanent.

The armor of God is His outline for your physical and spiritual protection. So, before you move forward in this book as it guides you to attack the hot buttons of bullying head-on, I want to lead you through a symbolic application of the armor of God.

It's very important that you don't glaze over or skip ahead. This is a great exercise to help you visualize the armor of God available for you and at work in your life. By physically displaying your reliance on that armor, you're stepping out in faith, believing that God's protection and provision are sufficient to meet your needs and your teens' needs. I do hope you'll take this section seriously even if you feel a little silly at times. It's not meant to be a trite exercise; it's a physical display of your faith in God's power and a symbol of your acceptance of His protections.

Below, you'll find a breakdown of Ephesians 6:10–17. Each phrase is followed by a bit of commentary and application, and a few directions.

Be strong in the Lord and in his mighty power. (Eph. 6:10)

This is an important assurance for families. You are not alone. All of the strength and wisdom you need to be a godly parent is already yours through the power of the Lord. And all of the power your tween or teen needs to withstand pressure and stand strong in the face of bullying is available. You don't have to have all of the answers—He does. You don't have to see the future—He does. You don't have to make up for the past—He did.

Do this: Raise your open hands in surrender, ready to receive from God, and expectant that He'll grant you strength, wisdom, and grace as you walk your children through the minefield of relationships.

Pray this: *Lord, please help me to place my faith firmly in You. Help me give up control, and surrender my family to You. Let me rest in Your power, and walk in Your strength. Guide my senses with Your knowledge and help me to know what I need to, when I need to, especially as it pertains to my kids and bullies.*

Put on the full armor of God, so that you can take your stand against the devil's schemes. (Eph. 6:11)

God has already provided protection for you and your kids. He's already secured your ultimate victory in the parenting battle—even if it seems daunting at times. Remember the promise in Philippians 1:6, where it says that He started the work (in your teens), and He'll finish it. He stands ready to uphold you as you face the enemy that seeks to pull your teens down a slippery slope.

Do this: Gird your shoulders; plant your feet. Stand proud like a soldier waiting for orders. Ultimately, as parents we are constantly waiting for divine direction, like a soldier ready to face any enemy in any battle.

Pray this: *Prepare my body to receive Your armor. Place it carefully that I might be protected as a parent from doubt, fear, and other attacks of the enemy as my kids go out into the world and face bullies of all kinds. Then, protect my teens in the same way, Father—their eyes, hands, mouths, and bodies . . . keep them physically safe and grant them wisdom as they deal with people.*

For **our struggle is not against flesh and blood**, but against the rulers, against the authorities, against the powers of this dark world and **against the spiritual forces of evil** in the heavenly realms. (Eph. 6:12)

You see, your real fight isn't against the bully. It isn't against the cliques. And it isn't against your teen's insecurities or self-image struggles. It's against the enemy who seeks to destroy in whatever way he can.

The Armor of God

Do this: Place your hands on your son's or daughter's bedroom door.

Pray this: *Father, I surrender this child, whom You love with a passion far greater than mine, to You. I call on Your mighty power to fight against our enemy who has no place among this family. We choose this day whom we will serve and I claim Your promises over the inhabitants of this home that no bullying stronghold will come against us.*

Therefore put on **the full armor of God**, so that when **the day of evil comes**, you may be able to **stand your ground**, and after you have done everything, to stand. (Eph. 6:13)

Armor puts a barricade around your heart, mind, and body to protect you from the attacks of the enemy. With the armor of God in place, Satan is ultimately powerless against you, and by extension, your teenagers, because we know how the story ends. It might seem like we lose some battles along the way; we might get discouraged at times. But, in the end, we win! We can rest in God's promises of ultimate victory and stand firm without fear. Even against the biggest bullies.

Do this: Close your eyes and imagine impenetrable steel covering every inch of your body and your child's body.

Pray this: *With armor in place, I stand proud as a soldier fighting for my family. I visualize the armor covering my child's head, heart, and soul. I stand confident in Your promises.*

> Stand firm then, with **the belt of truth** buckled around your waist . . . (Eph. 6:14a)

During times of battle, the tunic was belted to secure the soldier's clothes and keep every part of the armor in place, allowing him to move more freely. Without it, he would drop his shield or lose his helmet. In much the same way, the truth of the Word acts as a belt that keeps your armor in place as you stand against your enemy. It will keep all of His protection in place for you and for your kids as you navigate choices, fears, and hurts.

Do this: Buckle a proverbial belt around your waist. Then do the same in front of you as though your teen(s) are present.

Pray this: *With Your truth around our waists, help us harness the power in Your Word so we can stand against any enemy, confident in who we are in Your name.*

> . . . with the **breastplate of righteousness** in place . . . (Eph. 6:14b)

The breastplate provides protection for the heart and lungs, and without it, a solider is asking for death. A good breastplate wards off the attacks of the enemy, just as righteousness wards off the attacks of Satan.

Do this: Symbolically don the breastplate; then place it on your kids.

Pray this: *Let Your righteousness, Lord, be a shield about this family. Our protector and the lifter of our heads. Let Your armor shield my kids from the bullies who lurk in dark corners and the ones who shout from the rooftops.*

. . . and with your **feet fitted with the readiness** that comes **from the gospel of peace**. (Eph. 6:15)

You're ready. You have the information you need and you're covered in prayer. In the next chapters, you're going to actually implement the principles of getting and staying battle ready.

Do this: Lift each foot and plant it down hard.

Pray this: *I am confident in Your Word, Lord. I believe that You have led me and prepared me to be my teens' very best advocate in this world. I am prepared to fight as Your ambassador, ready with Your Word to stand against any bully and to help my kids do the same.*

In addition to all this, **take up the shield of faith**, with which you can extinguish all the flaming arrows of the evil one. (Eph. 6:16)

Notice, the shield is active, not simply defensive. You're not blocking the enemy's arrows and sending them back out to do damage somewhere else, you're *extinguishing* them. Apply that to the evil intentions of bullies. Pray that their efforts against your tweens and teens are extinguished before they hit their targets.

Do this: Raise your arm as though you hold a shield and wave it in front of you. Imagine your kids standing before you, and wave it in front of each of them also.

Pray this: *Put out the flames, Lord. Let this shield of my faith swallow them whole that they would disappear, never to harm another soul again.*

Take the **helmet of salvation** . . . (Eph. 6:17a)

The helmet of salvation protects our minds from sin, doubt, fear, and other cares of this world. It's the promise of eternity. With the helmet securely fastened, we walk free with the understanding that the trials of this world are temporary. No matter what we face, we can take refuge in the assurance of our salvation.

Do this: Place the helmet of salvation securely over your head, to your shoulders. Reach out in front of you and do the same as though your teens stood before you.

Pray this: *I rest in my salvation, Lord. You are mighty to save and faithful to preserve.*

. . . and the **sword of the Spirit**, which is the word of God. (Eph. 6:17b)

You're armed and ready to fight. In the following chapters, I will walk you through the next action steps in your battle for your tweens and teens.

Do this: Raise your sword, which is the Bible—the Word of God.

Pray this: *I am equipped through Your Word, ready to fight Satan's schemes against my kids. I need You to guide me and show me what my next move should be. Keep my heart and mind open to the truths and possibilities of what my kids face. And help them, Lord, to have the strength to say no, the wisdom to walk away, and the passion to chase hard after You. Amen.*

———————————

Strategic
Scenarios

The first few chapters of this book identified why it's necessary to press the hot buttons with your tweens and teens about bullying and all that comes along with that topic. Part 2 outlined the specific segments of the issues like insecurity, cliques, cyberbullying, popularity, self-harm, and more. Now it's time to help your kids develop skills that will affect real change and have a lasting impact on their relationships and their choices.

Everyone wants to be liked and to have a lot of friends. Acceptance is one of the natural desires of human nature. It isn't going away, and it can't be ignored. Opportunistic people capitalize on those desires and bullying behaviors begin. It's a slippery slope and so difficult to end once it's begun. Don't leave this one to chance while you hope for the best, parents. Invest time in conversations with your children and reap the rewards.

Working through the Strategic Scenarios will involve putting your tween or teen into a scenario by telling a short story. You'll then present a few optional responses to the situation from which you'll allow your child to choose the most natural personal choice without any judgment. Once that decision is made, you'll be guided through several discussion points, and referred back to material given previously in this book.

Each discussion will end with the opportunity for your son or daughter to change the initial decision that was made and commit to wise choices in the future.

Some of the scenarios are written from the perspective of a particular gender. You should still guide your tween or teen through them, either modifying the situation to match your child's gender, or helping him or her see the particular difficulties experienced by the opposite gender. Don't skip over the ones that don't seem to apply right away. Every scenario can help your kids to observe the world through the eyes of Christ, and to be prepared to act in a way that would please Him.

Strategic Scenario 1

Parents, tell your teen this story.

You had to stay after class to ask your teacher a question, so you arrive a few minutes late to lunch. The lunchroom is packed and the tables all look full. There are plenty of seats at the tables where the popular kids sit, but you wouldn't dare try to sit with them. You stand in the middle of the room with your tray. Why doesn't someone offer you a seat? What do you do?

Now offer the following options with no personal commentary.

Let your teen think about the choices and make an honest decision.

A. You dump your food in the garbage and head to your next class. You weren't very hungry anyway.

B. Your lower lip starts to quiver, and you just know tears are on the way. You run out and hide in the bathroom.

C. You slump over to a random table and ask the students there to move down a few inches so you can perch on the edge of the bench long enough to choke down your grilled cheese.

D. You go ahead and sit in the empty spot at the popular table. They only get away with that kind of exclusivity because other kids give them that kind of power.

Crucial step

Use this scenario to guide a discussion about confidence. Be very careful not to sound judgmental or accusatory as you discuss the options. Remember, your teen is exploring thoughts and first impressions—these aren't actual choices . . . yet.

Discussion Points

- Why did you make the choice you did?
- What's the worst that could happen?
- Do you have the confidence to stand up against exclusivity? Why or why not?
- What kind of friend is Jesus?
- What are some of the possible outcomes of this scenario?
- What will you do the next time you see someone searching for a seat?
- What if it's the most unpopular kid in school? The most popular?
- Do you now have a different view on this scenario than you did at the start? Why or why not?
- Would you like to change your answer or stick with it?

For the Spirit God gave us does not make us timid, **but gives us power**, love and self-discipline.

(2 Tim. 1:7)

Parents, tell your teen this story.

Over a long weekend, a couple of guys from the football team make up a fake email account using the name of one of the geeky, unpopular boys in school. Using that account, they send letters and pictures to the cheerleaders, pledging his undying love. You tried to stop them—kind of. But they didn't take you seriously. They then print the emails, planning to sneak into school a little early on Monday morning to put them in lockers and throughout the school. They assume you're going to help since you were there for the whole thing. What do you do?

Now offer the following options with no personal commentary.

Let your teen think about the choices and make an honest decision.

A. You tell your friends you're not going to help and they should stop immediately and send a confession letter to all the girls who got an email.

B. You laugh it off and tell your friends you can't get there early. They can do it without you, but they don't need to know you don't approve.

C. You might as well help them. You sure don't want them turning on you.

D. You alert the school administration to what is expected to happen, and then you call the victim and tell him what happened so he and his parents can be prepared for Monday morning.

Crucial Step

Use this scenario to guide a discussion about defending the underdog. Be very careful not to sound judgmental or accusatory. Remember, your teen is exploring thoughts and first impressions—these aren't actual choices . . . yet.

Discussion Points

- Why did you make the choice you did?
- Where did this situation first go wrong?
- What could have been done at the first hint of wrongdoing?
- How could you use this opportunity to share the love of Jesus with others?
- What kind of person does God call you to be?
- What kind of friends do you want to have?
- What is more important: popularity or integrity?
- Do you now have a different view on this scenario than you did at the start? Why or why not?
- Would you like to change your answer or stick with it?

Keep your tongue from evil and your lips from telling lies. **Turn from evil and do good**; seek peace and pursue it.

(Ps. 34:13–14)

Parents, tell your teen this story.

You notice that a close friend of yours has been skipping classes on a pretty regular basis, even missing whole days of school, supposedly sick. You do a little digging and find out she's avoiding a specific person. Further questioning reveals that she's been receiving threats and insults from this other student. Your friend refuses to go to the school administration or tell her parents because she fears the threats and bullying will just get worse. Or that something bad will actually happen to her. She asks you to promise you won't say anything. What do you do?

Now offer the following options with no personal commentary.

Let your teen think about the choices and make an honest decision.

> A. You talk to your parents about it and let them decide what to do.
> B. Ignore it. It's not your problem.
> C. You honor her wishes. You sure don't want to get involved and cause her more problems than she already has or get the focus turned to you.
> D. You don't break her confidence, but you do try to convince your friend to stand up against the bully.

Crucial Step

Use this scenario to guide a discussion about keeping quiet about bullying. Be very careful not to sound judgmental or accusatory. Remember, your teen is exploring thoughts and first impressions—these aren't actual choices . . . yet.

Discussion Points

- Why did you make the choice you did?
- When is it necessary to break a confidence?
- Under what circumstances would it be okay to keep a secret like this?
- How could you help your friend immediately?
- What would you do if you were in her shoes?
- What are some ways you could share God's love in this situation?
- Do you now have a different view on this scenario than you did at the start? Why or why not?
- Would you like to change your answer or stick with it?

Rescue the weak and the needy; **deliver them from** the hand of **the wicked**.

(Ps. 82:4)

Parents, tell your teen this story.

Your friends are always slamming kids of other races and use really bad names to describe them. They do this privately, but it's pretty clear that they shun anyone who doesn't look just like they do. One of these days, they're going to take it too far and really hurt someone's feelings. And what if people think you agree with them? What do you do?

Now offer the following options with no personal commentary.

Let your teen think about the choices and make an honest decision.

> A. They don't mean any harm, and they really are kind of funny. You just laugh along with them once in a while.
>
> B. You tell your friends that they have to stop talking like that around you.
>
> C. You can't be friends with those kids any longer. You can't condone that kind of hate. Even if they don't say it around you, it's still who they are.
>
> D. As long as they only say that stuff in private, it's not your concern. You let your friends know that you're worried about people overhearing them, and ask them to be careful.

Crucial Step

Use this scenario to guide a discussion about prejudice. Be very careful not to sound judgmental or accusatory. Remember, your teen is exploring thoughts and first impressions—these aren't actual choices . . . yet.

Discussion Points

- Why did you make the choice you did?
- What kinds of people do you want to have as friends?
- How does your choice in friends reflect on you personally?
- Do you see this kind of behavior in your school?
- Read chapter 4 to learn about various perceived weaknesses that bullies target.
- How does Jesus feel about different kinds of people?
- Do you want to be a strong, confident person, or do you want to be a follower and a people-pleaser even if it means hurting others?
- Do you now have a different view on this scenario than you did at the start? Why or why not?
- Would you like to change your answer or stick with it?

Do not let any unwholesome talk come out of your mouths, but **only what is helpful for building others up** according to their needs, that it may benefit those who listen. (Eph. 4:29)

Strategic Scenario 5

Parents, tell your teen this story.

In the same month you got braces put on your teeth, you started wearing glasses, and your skin broke out in acne. You're being teased mercilessly and things are changing for you. It seems like your friends aren't hanging out with you as much—they probably don't want to be in the line of fire. You try to smile through it all and pray it ends soon, but what if it doesn't? What do you do?

Now offer the following options with no personal commentary.

Let your teen think about the choices and make an honest decision.

> A. You fight back with insults of your own. You show them you aren't going to take it.
>
> B. You talk to a teacher and to your parents. They'll find a way to make it stop.
>
> C. You ignore the jabs. Eventually the bullies will tire of getting no response from you.
>
> D. You try to talk to them about the effect their insults have on you and ask for a truce.

Crucial Step

Use this scenario to guide a discussion about handling bullies. Be very careful not to sound judgmental or accusatory. Remember, your teen is exploring thoughts and first impressions—these aren't actual choices . . . yet.

Discussion Points

- Why did you make the choice you did?
- How would you feel in this situation?
- Do you know students who actually have to deal with this scenario?
- Would you feel comfortable talking with Mom or Dad if you found yourself in a situation like this? Why or why not?
- How would you want your parents to help you with this?
- Parents, read *Hot Buttons Image Edition* to help with conversations about body image and self-esteem.
- Do you now have a different view on this scenario than you did at the start? Why or why not?
- Would you like to change your answer or stick with it?

You have heard people say, "Love your neighbors and hate your enemies." But I tell you to **love your enemies and pray for anyone who mistreats you**. Then you will be acting like your Father in heaven.

(Matt. 5:43–45 CEV)

Parents, tell your teen this story.

You're walking down the school hallway with your friend from youth group. Four mean girls corner you at the end of the hallway. This isn't the first time—but it seems like it's getting worse each time. The leader of the group pins your friend against a locker and rifles through her backpack. You try to keep the begging tone from your voice as you ask them to please just leave you alone. The leader turns a cold stare to you. "You want us to leave you alone?" She yanks the Bible out of your friend's backpack and holds it high. "All you have to do is tell us that this is a bunch of lies and you don't believe it at all." You're desperate for the bullying to stop. What do you do?

Now offer the following options with no personal commentary.

Let your teen think about the choices and make an honest decision.

> A. Words are nothing but words. You say what they want to hear.
> B. You try to reason with them and stall until the bell rings. That will at least buy you some time until you can talk to your parents.
> C. You stand up straight. "Jesus Christ is my Lord and Savior. There is nothing you can do to me that would make me deny that."
> D. You run away. Your friend can handle herself.

Crucial Step

Use this scenario to guide a discussion about defending faith. Be very careful not to sound judgmental or accusatory. Remember, your teen is exploring thoughts and first impressions—these aren't actual choices . . . yet.

Discussion Points

* Why did you make the choice you did?
* Do words matter?
* What are some ways you could use this situation to share God's love?
* Why would bullies care about your faith?
* Are you really as powerless and out of control as bullies want you to believe?
* How confident are you in defending your faith?
* What does Jesus want you to do?
* Do you now have a different view on this scenario than you did at the start? Why or why not?
* Would you like to change your answer or stick with it?

Everyone **who acknowledges me publicly** here on earth, **I will also acknowledge before my Father in heaven**. But everyone who denies me here on earth, I will also deny before my Father in heaven. (Matt. 10:32–33 NLT)

Parents, tell your teen this story.

Your neighbor is an old friend even though you don't hang out at school very much. You heard his parents are going through a divorce, and that he's been having a hard time with everything. It seems like he's neglected his schoolwork, he's wearing all black, and he has gotten a few piercings. You've overheard some other kids picking on him. Yesterday, you happened upon a scene where he was pushed to the ground, kicked in the stomach, and someone even spit in his face. Just a bit ago, you logged into one of your social network accounts and saw where he posted anonymously that he'd be better off dead. Problem is, no one else knows that's his account. What do you do?

Now offer the following options with no personal commentary.

Let your teen think about the choices and make an honest decision.

> A. You don't want to embarrass him, so you log out and leave him to his privacy. If he wanted you to know how he felt, he'd tell you.
>
> B. You reach out to him and let him know you're there for him, praying for him. You apologize for not coming to his rescue when people were bullying him, and promise to back him up next time.
>
> C. You talk to your parents and show them the online post. Someone needs to help him.
>
> D. You stick around to keep an eye on him, but you stay out of it. If it gets worse, you'll do something.

Crucial Step

Use this scenario to begin a discussion about depression, bullying, and suicide. Be very careful not to sound judgmental or accusatory. Remember, your teen is exploring thoughts and first impressions—these aren't actual choices . . . yet.

Discussion Points

- Why did you make the choice you did?
- What is the progression that leads to suicidal thoughts?
- Is suicide or depression glamorized in your school?
- Should threats or comments like that ever be ignored?
- At what point should this boy have gotten help?
- Who would you turn to in a tough situation like this?
- Parents, this may be a good time to discuss some tips from *Hot Buttons Internet Edition*.
- Do you now have a different view on this scenario than you did at the start? Why or why not?
- Would you like to change your answer or stick with it?

The Spirit of the Lord is on me, because **he has anointed me to proclaim good news** to the poor. He has sent me to proclaim freedom for the prisoners and recovery of sight for the blind, **to set the oppressed free**, to proclaim the year of the Lord's favor.

(Luke 4:18–19)

Strategic Scenario 8

Parents, tell your teen this story.

Now that you're in middle school, you have to change into gym clothes before gym class every day. An overweight girl tries to hide behind her locker door or goes into the bathroom stall to change. You can hardly blame her because the other girls call her names and laugh at her. One girl just took a quick picture of the mostly naked student and is now threatening to text it to some of the boys. What do you do?

Now offer the following options with no personal commentary.

Let your teen think about the choices and make an honest decision.

> A. No way you're getting involved in this. They'll just turn on you if you do. You pretend you have no idea what's happening.
>
> B. You grab the phone from the girl's hand and delete the picture before she can stop you.
>
> C. You tell a teacher immediately.
>
> D. You can't stop what's happening, but you'll at least try to be nice to the lonely girl later.

Crucial Step

Use this scenario to guide a discussion about cyberbullying. Be very careful not to sound judgmental or accusatory. Remember, your teen is exploring thoughts and first impressions—these aren't actual choices . . . yet.

Discussion Points

- Why did you make the choice you did?
- What are some words that could describe how this girl would feel in that situation?
- What are some practical ways you could help her get through the embarrassment of gym class?
- How could you show her the love of Jesus?
- Can pictures actually be deleted off a cell phone?
- Would it make a difference in how you would react if the girl with the phone was a popular girl?
- Read chapter 7 in this book along with *Hot Buttons Image Edition* to learn about how this kind of bullying can lead to eating disorders and other forms of self-harm.
- See the recommended resources section for hotlines and information about bullying.
- Do you now have a different view on this scenario than you did at the start? Why or why not?
- Would you like to change your answer or stick with it?

Be fair to the poor and to orphans. **Defend the helpless** and everyone in need.
(Ps. 82:3 CEV)

Parents, tell your teen this story.

There's a new girl in school and she's already become a target for the bullies. You've heard about some things that have happened to her, but you have no real proof. She does seem really sad, though. Today, you're behind her in the lunch line waiting for her to balance her tray and her book bag. In her maneuvering, her sleeve comes up and you see rows of cuts up her forearm, some old, some very fresh. She hurriedly covers her arm, but not before she locks eyes with you. You open your mouth to say something, but she darts away. What do you do?

Now offer the following options with no personal commentary.

Let your teen think about the choices and make an honest decision.

> A. You find an opportunity to talk to her alone and let her know you're there to talk if she needs to.
>
> B. You make it a point to find her the next day and invite her to sit with you at lunch.
>
> C. You don't even know this girl, what can you do? You let it go and go sit with your friends.
>
> D. You talk to a parent or school counselor and let them know about the bullying and the cutting.

Crucial Step

Use this scenario to begin a discussion about self-harm. Be very careful not to sound judgmental or accusatory. Remember, your teen is exploring thoughts and first impressions—these aren't actual choices . . . yet.

Discussion Points

- Why did you make the choice you did?
- What is self-harm?
- Discuss chapter 7 for more help with the subjects of cutting, suicide, eating disorders, and other forms of self-harm.
- What are some possible signs of self-harm?
- Being a relative stranger to this girl, what would your responsibility be?
- What if you did nothing?
- How could you show God's love to those around you in this situation?
- Do you now have a different view on this scenario than you did at the start? Why or why not?
- Would you like to change your answer or stick with it?

Children, you **show love for others by truly helping them**, and not merely by talking about it.
(1 John 3:18 CEV)

Parents, tell your teen this story.

Your favorite subject is science. You love all the experiments and discussions. In fact, you just might go after some aspect of a career in science. Something's bothering you, though. Your teacher has been teaching evolution and some of it makes sense, but you believe that God created the earth and everything in it. Your teacher taunts you and asks you to defend your position in front of the whole class. You can't argue with her—she knows her stuff—but you know what you believe is true. It's getting so bad that you're nauseous before class every day. What do you do?

Now offer the following options with no personal commentary.

Let your teen think about the choices and make an honest decision.

> A. You have a talk with your teacher and let her know how her public taunting hurts you.
>
> B. You just skip class. You don't need to deal with that.
>
> C. You get a bunch of your friends together and figure out various ways to make your teacher miserable.
>
> D. You talk with your parents and ask them to go to the school administration to make sure nothing like this happens again, to you or someone else.

Crucial Step

Use this scenario to begin a discussion about the issue of being bullied by those in authority. Be very careful not to sound judgmental or accusatory. Remember, your teen is exploring thoughts and first impressions—these aren't actual choices . . . yet.

Discussion Points

- Why did you make the choice you did?
- Is this scenario bullying? Why or why not?
- Discuss chapter 4 on perceived weaknesses. Who is the weaker person in this scenario?
- Are there other ways you could handle this, besides the four options provided?
- How can you show proper resect to adults if they are mistreating you?
- How important is it to be able to defend your faith?
- How could you use this situation to share God's truth with others?
- Do you now have a different view on this scenario than you did at the start? Why or why not?
- Would you like to change your answer or stick with it?

Always **be prepared to give an answer** to everyone who asks you **to give the reason for the hope that you have**. But do this with gentleness and respect.

(1 Peter 3:15)

Parents, tell your teen this story.

A group of the most popular boys in school has been picking on one of the kids from the special education class. They keep telling this boy to do things that are bad or dangerous and then video record what happens. When this boy does what he's told, the boys laugh and make fun of him. The boy doesn't seem to realize that they're laughing at him, and he laughs and smiles, thinking they're being friendly. The videos keep ending up on Facebook and some other websites. You're not a part of the boys' group, but you're still friends with them. What do you do?

Now offer the following options with no personal commentary.

Let your teen think about the choices and make an honest decision.

A. At least the boy doesn't realize what's happening. Since it's not really hurting him, you stay out of it.

B. Whether he realizes it or not, you can't just keep letting this kid get made fun of. You step in and say something to the boys.

C. You talk to the boys and tell them to at least stop making the boy do things that could get him hurt.

D. He could seriously get hurt one day, plus, videos on the Internet are permanent. His parents need to know about this. You tell them right away.

Crucial Step

Use this scenario to guide a discussion about standing up for those who are weaker. Be very careful not to sound judgmental or accusatory. Remember, your teen is exploring thoughts and first impressions—these aren't actual choices . . . yet.

Discussion Points

- Why did you make the choice you did?
- Parents, discuss chapter 4.
- Do you see things like this happen at school?
- How does it make you feel?
- What are some other ways you could help in this situation?
- How would Jesus have treated this boy?
- What are some ways you could use this situation to show God's love?
- Do you now have a different view on this scenario than you did at the start? Why or why not?
- Would you like to change your answer or stick with it?

Speak up for those who cannot speak for themselves, for the rights of all who are destitute. Speak up and judge fairly; **defend the rights of the poor and needy**. (Prov. 31:8–9)

Parents, tell your teen this story.

You moved this year and had to start at a new middle school. Pretty, athletic, and funny, you get attention from some of the football players, which doesn't make the cheerleaders very happy. They band together to create a Facebook page where they post horrible lies about you, call you fat, and other gross things. Word gets around school and others join in by liking the page and posting even more hurtful things. Maybe you are a little overweight, and if you lose a few pounds, then they won't be able to call you fat anymore, and then maybe you'll make the cheer squad next year. You begin to take diet pills and even make yourself throw up after a few meals. Now what do you do?

Now offer the following options with no personal commentary.

Let your teen think about the choices and make an honest decision.

A. You fight back, posting hateful responses to your attackers on the Facebook page.

B. Maybe if you make a couple of close friends, you'll feel better. You join a sport.

C. Skinny is best. You do everything you can to get supermodel thin. That should do it.

D. You're not going to let them bully you into unhealthy behaviors any longer. You turn to your mom for help.

Crucial Step

Use this scenario to guide a discussion about eating disorders and self-harm. Be very careful not to sound judgmental or accusatory. Remember, your teen is exploring thoughts and first impressions—these aren't actual choices . . . yet.

Discussion Points

- Why did you make the choice you did?
- How can bullying of this type cause a teenager to make unhealthy choices?
- Read chapter 7 on self-harm and *Hot Buttons Image Edition* for more help on these issues.
- Listening to lies from bullies can often make you see flaws in yourself that don't exist.
- How does God see you?
- Why would anyone want to join up with their tormentors?
- What are some ways you could use this situation to share God's love with your abusers?
- Do you now have a different view on this scenario than you did at the start? Why or why not?
- Would you like to change your answer or stick with it?

The LORD does not look at the things people look at. People look at the outward appearance, but **the LORD looks at the heart**.

(1 Sam. 16:7)

Parents, tell your teen this story.

You and some friends meet by the high school flagpole once a week for prayer. Some of the more popular kids think you're all fake, and they try to find ways to show that you're not for real. They spread rumors on the Internet and manufacture photos of you all drinking at a party. With your reputation at stake, maybe you should stop being so open about your faith. Maybe then you'd be less of a target. What do you do?

Now offer the following options with no personal commentary.

Let your teen think about the choices and make an honest decision.

A. You bring this to the attention of school administrators. Those kids should be punished for what they're doing, and you don't want fake pictures of you drinking to get you kicked off the tennis team.

B. You lay low for a while. You don't have to pray in public for God to hear you.

C. You let the rumors happen. Maybe their plan will backfire and it will just make you more popular!

D. You keep right on doing what you're doing, knowing that persecution comes when people stand up for Christ.

Crucial Step

Use this scenario to guide a discussion about persecution for the cause of Christ. Be very careful not to sound judgmental or accusatory. Remember, your teen is exploring thoughts and first impressions—these aren't actual choices . . . yet.

Discussion Points

- Why did you make the choice you did?
- What does it mean to turn the other cheek?
- Do you have to sit back and take all sorts of abuse?
- Is it okay to fight back?
- How would Jesus respond to these attackers?
- Would you tell your parents? Why or why not?
- Do you now have a different view on this scenario than you did at the start? Why or why not?
- Would you like to change your answer or stick with it?

Blessed are those who are persecuted because of righteousness, for theirs is the kingdom of heaven. Blessed are you when people insult you, persecute you and falsely say all kinds of evil against you because of me. **Rejoice and be glad, because great is your reward in heaven.**

(Matt. 5:10–12)

Parents, tell your teen this story.

A kid you know committed suicide a few months ago. You weren't exactly friends, but you did know he got picked on a lot and spent most of his time alone. You didn't ever join in with the bullying, but you never did anything to try to stop it, either. You've been feeling like maybe you're responsible for his death, at least partly. What do you do?

Now offer the following options with no personal commentary.

Let your teen think about the choices and make an honest decision.

A. There's nothing you can do. You move on.

B. You go to the boy's parents and apologize for not standing up for their son when you had the chance. You commit to them that you will work to end bullying in your school.

C. You make a commitment to be more aware of people who are hurting, but you sure don't want anyone to know you feel guilty about this.

D. You begin to talk to other kids, especially the bullies, about how abusive behavior can cause kids to feel hopeless and want to escape.

Crucial Step

Use this scenario to guide a discussion about the permanent effects of bullying. Be very careful not to sound judgmental or accusatory. Remember, your teen is exploring thoughts and first impressions—these aren't actual choices . . . yet.

Discussion Points

- Why did you make the choice you did?
- Parents, discuss chapter 7 about self-harm.
- How far does your responsibility go in this scenario?
- How would you feel if this happened and you'd done nothing?
- What steps could have been taken that would have prevented any feelings of guilt in this scenario?
- Would God hold you responsible for this?
- Might those steps have also prevented the suicide?
- See the recommended resources section for help in dealing with suicide.
- Do you now have a different view on this scenario than you did at the start? Why or why not?
- Would you like to change your answer or stick with it?

"For **I know the plans I have for you**," declares the LORD, "plans to prosper you and not to harm you, **plans to give you hope and a future**."
(Jer. 29:11)

Parents, tell your teen this story.

You've been moving up the popularity chain lately—and it's tons of fun. You're sitting at the cool table at lunch and getting invited to the best parties. You don't have much time for your old friends anymore, but that's a small price to pay for popularity like this. But one of your old BFFs keeps trying to hang out. Your new friends wrote a note to her, telling her she isn't cool enough for you so you can't hang out with her. They told you to sign it, so you did. They're about to give it to her. What do you do?

Now offer the following options with no personal commentary.

Let your teen think about the choices and make an honest decision.

A. You didn't write it, and you don't want to upset these cool kids. Hopefully your ex-BFF will understand.

B. You quickly scribble a note explaining yourself to your old friend. You'll give it to her later when the others aren't around.

C. You look the other way. You do kind of want her off your back. Maybe this will work.

D. You rush over to the table where your new friends are about to give her the note. You grab it and tear it up.

Crucial Step

Use this scenario to guide a discussion about the intentions behind bullying and the price of popularity. Be very careful not to sound judgmental or accusatory. Remember, your teen is exploring thoughts and first impressions—these aren't actual choices . . . yet.

Discussion Points

- Why did you make the choice you did?
- Does bullying always have to be intentional?
- How does this situation look and feel from the perspective of the old BFF?
- Which is more important: treating others as Jesus would, or being popular?
- Many would say this is silly social stuff, not bullying. What do you think?
- Can you think of options other than the ones listed?
- Do you now have a different view on this scenario than you did at the start? Why or why not?
- Would you like to change your answer or stick with it?

Treat others as you want them to treat you. This is what the Law and the Prophets are all about. (Matt. 7:12 CEV)

PART FOUR

Parent-Teen STUDY GUIDE

Congratulations on making it this far through *Hot Buttons Bullying Edition!* This book dealt with some tough issues and walked you through the practice of using Strategic Scenarios to prepare your teens for issues related to bullying and some of the self-esteem problems that can result. Now we're going to press in a little deeper and do some work on the spiritual side of choices: sin, confession, and forgiveness.

Whether your child is the victim, the bully, or neither, confession, forgiveness, and grace are applicable to all of life. Work through these studies individually, then come together to discuss your findings. If you've already worked through these study chapters in another Hot Buttons book, please do them again. There's no better way to really learn, really internalize something than to repeat it. You might want to pull them out every six months or year to see if things have changed and to make sure you're still on the same page.

Visit www.hotbuttonsite.com/study-guide to find a downloadable and printable version of this study guide in which space for writing is included, so everyone can have a copy for personal study.

chapter 12

Confession

Very **truly I tell you**, the one who **believes** has eternal life. (John 6:47)

. . . **Jesus is the Messiah**, the Son of God, and that **by believing** you may have life in his name. (John 20:31)

Jesus said to her, "I am the resurrection and the life. The one **who believes in me will live**, even though they die; and whoever lives by believing in me will never die. Do you *believe* this?" (John 11:25–26)

If you **confess with your mouth Jesus as Lord**, and **believe in your heart** that God raised Him from the dead, **you will be saved**; for with the heart a person *believes*, resulting in righteousness, and with the mouth he confesses, resulting in salvation. (Rom. 10:9–10 NASB)

◀According to these verses, what is required for salvation?

Stop and think. Have you confessed with your mouth and believed in your heart that Jesus is Lord? Share the answer with your study partner(s).

◀What does that mean to you to have made that choice?

If you haven't done that but would like to now, take a walk through the following Scriptures. If you're a Christian already, it's still a good exercise to look at these foundational truths as a refresher.

◀Read Romans 3:23. Who has sinned?

◀Read Romans 6:23a. What is the price of sin?

Sin requires a penalty. The only payment for it is death, blood. Worse than a physical death, though, is the spiritual death that separates us from God for eternity.

◀Read Romans 6:23b. What is God's gift?

◀Read Romans 5:8. How much does God love you?

Jesus gave His own life on the cross to pay the penalty for all of our sin. He, an innocent man, took your death sentence and stood in your place, giving you new life in exchange for His death.

◀Read Romans 10:13 and Revelation 3:20. Who qualifies for salvation?

If you'd like to welcome Jesus into your life and receive the free gift of eternal life that He offers, simply pray this prayer:

> *Dear Jesus, I believe in You. I believe that You are the Son of God and my Savior and Lord. I ask You to forgive my sins and make*

Confession

me clean. Please help me do the right thing, but I thank You for the forgiveness You offer me when I mess up. I give my life to You. Amen.

If you took that step, *congratulations*!

Everything pales in comparison to the choice to walk with Jesus through your life. Now we can apply that choice of confession to the issues in this book and to your relationships.

> Therefore **confess your sins** to each other and pray for each other so that you may be healed. The **prayer of a righteous person is powerful** and effective. (James 5:16)

Confessing your sins *to others* is not a requirement of salvation. James 5 doesn't suggest that you should confess your sins to each other so that you might be saved. Confession to God is the only path to salvation. James 5 is referring instead to healing of the mind, the mending of broken trust, and the repairing of damaged relationships that only come about by seeking forgiveness from those you have wronged in the past.

Confession clears the air and allows forgiveness to blossom where bitterness once festered. And confession carries healing power no matter what the response is. In other words, your confession starts the healing process in you, regardless of how it's received or if forgiveness is immediately granted.

◀ Work together to write a description of the purpose of confession in family relationships.

Though forgiveness in Christ is complete, sin continues to thrive in the darkness of secrecy. Confession to a loved one deflates sin's power like the air rushing out of a balloon. The sin shrivels, its grip releases, and its power dies. What was once a tool of the enemy to destroy you and your family is now a bonding agent that unites and builds strength and character. What a victory!

When is it important to confess to each other?

- ◀ When the issue is causing division
- ◀ When there is bitterness
- ◀ When you're unable to find peace
- ◀ When you need forgiveness

Now is the time to take a risk. You've confessed to God, and you're forgiven of your sins because of the death and resurrection of God's Son, Jesus. Now it's time to lay your heart bare before your loved ones. Trust that we'll get to the forgiveness part of this study just as soon as you turn the page. Let go of the fear of admitting your faults. Confess today so you can be forgiven and see your relationships restored once and for all.

Open your heart and mind, and let the Holy Spirit reveal the things that you need to let out. Let this be a safe moment in your family in which you feel free to lay your heart bare and free your spirit of any guilt or condemnation that binds you.

◀ Take this time to confess whatever the Lord is bringing to your mind. You may verbalize your confession, or write it in your own notebook or in your study guide (which you can find at www.hotbuttonsite.com).

Trust that your loved ones' response to your confession will be one of forgiveness—the next chapter will lead you through that.

Parent's Prayer

Father, I confess the times I've failed as a parent and ask You to forgive me and help me have more self-control and wisdom when I respond to things. Please help me to be a godly example and a role model for my kids. Give us the kind of relationship that mirrors the one You have with us. Thank You for Your example of unconditional love, continual acceptance, and constant approachability. Make me that kind of parent, and help my family to forgive me for the times I haven't been. Amen.

Teen's Prayer

Dear God, please forgive me for not respecting my parents all the time. Help me to honor the values we've decided upon as a family and uphold them in all things. Give me the strength to say no to the pressure I'm placed under to do all sorts of wrong things. Please help me to be a better son/daughter and make us a loving and united family that serves You together. Amen.

13 Forgiveness

Following belief and confession is forgiveness. Ah, what a blessed state to live in . . . forgiven. The very word elicits a sense of peace and calm. It inspires me to take a deep breath and rest for a moment in gratitude.

How about you? Do you feel forgiven?

> If we **confess our sins**, he is faithful and just and will **forgive us** our sins and **purify us** from all unrighteousness. (1 John 1:9)

Do you believe that you're forgiven? Sometimes it hits like a tsunami as the waves of peace wash over the heart. For others, it's more of a steady rain that takes time to feel. It's okay, either way. Whether you feel forgiven or not, you can have faith that you are, in fact, purified and holy before God.

So God has forgiven you, but now what does He expect you to do about other people who have wronged you?

> For if you **forgive other people** when they sin against you,
> your **heavenly Father will also forgive you**. But if you
> do not forgive others their sins, your Father will not forgive your
> sins. (Matt. 6:14–15)

◀ What does that passage teach about forgiveness?

◀ How do you feel about that?

Forgiving others is often a simple act of obedience and a step of faith. If you're angry or wronged in some way, you're rarely going to feel like forgiving those who hurt you. Forgiveness, in that case, is a gift from God planted in your heart so that you might extend it toward those who sinned against you.

Would you be surprised if I told you that offering forgiveness benefits you far more than it benefits the person you're attempting to forgive? Surrendering in that way allows God to work more deeply in your life.

◀ Read Ephesians 4:25 and Luke 15. How do you think God wants us to receive someone's confession?

◀ Now, think about this question: Can you truly accept someone's confession and offer forgiveness without holding on to any bitterness or contempt?

◀ What makes that easy or difficult for you?

◀ Read Matthew 18:21–35. Who do the characters in this parable represent? What is the debt? What is the parable trying to show us?

> **Bear with each another** and forgive one another if any of you has a grievance against someone. **Forgive as the Lord forgave you**. And over all these virtues put on love, which binds them **all together in perfect unity**. (Col. 3:13–14)

Parents, name some times you've been forgiven of things in your life and share them here. Try for at least five examples. Spend as much time thinking about this as necessary.

When you see it written out like that, does it give you a different perspective on your teen's sins?

But I'm not God!

What about when it's just too bad, and I'm truly unable to let go of the anger toward someone?

> And when you stand praying, if you hold anything against anyone, **forgive them**, so that your Father in heaven may forgive you your sins. (Mark 11:25)

> Do not judge, and you will not be judged. Do not condemn, and you will not be condemned. **Forgive**, and you will be forgiven. (Luke 6:37)

Believe me, I get it. It's not easy to forgive those who have committed a painful wrong against you and are truly guilty. The problem is that unforgiveness drives a wedge into our daily walk with God. That free and open walk with a loving Savior becomes strained and even avoided when your spirit knows it's harboring something God cannot abide. He talked to His children about this specific issue because He doesn't want it to divide you from Him.

◀ Are you able to forgive each other for the things confessed before God in the last chapter? Are you able to treat those confessions with the same manner of grace that God has shown you? Is anything standing in your way? Take turns sharing.

We've made huge progress through confessing to God and each other, receiving God's grace, and forgiving others. I'd like to encourage you to backtrack a little and dig a little deeper.

◀ What are you still holding on to that needs to be confessed to your family? What sin still makes you cringe when you consider sharing it? Why can't you let it go?

Now's the time to take a chance. Forgiveness is a step away. Families, assure each other that it's safe to unload anything at this time. God has forgiven your sins, past, present, and future—now allow your family to do the same.

Confession followed by forgiveness is a life-changing gift of healing.

Parent's Prayer

Heavenly Father, I'm so grateful for Your grace and forgiveness. I'm so grateful that it extends to cover the mistakes I make as a Christian and as a parent. Please help me forgive others like You have forgiven me so that I can be an extension of Your arm of mercy to those around me. Let me show grace to my children so they will trust me with their sins and their feelings. Help me not to expect them to be perfect, but rather to see them as You see them and readily offer forgiveness at all times. Amen.

Teen's Prayer

Lord, I've done some dumb things—thank You for forgiving me for them. Your gift of salvation has changed my life, and I'm not the same person I was before You came into it. Thank You, too, for helping me and my family work through some of these things. It all makes sense when we talk about it and look at what the Bible says. Help me not to hold grudges against people who have hurt me, and help me to be obedient to You and to my parents. Please help me make good decisions and not to give in to peer pressure. Amen.

c h a p t e r

Clean Slate **14**

> For as **high as the heavens** are above the earth,
> **so great is his love** for those who fear him;
> as far as the east is from the west,
> so far has he **removed our transgressions** from us.
>
> (Ps. 103:11–12)

◀ In light of Psalm 103:11–12, what does the following quote mean to you?

> "I can forgive, but I cannot forget," is only another way of
> saying, "I will not forgive." Forgiveness ought to be like
> a cancelled note, torn in two, and burned up so it can
> never be shown against one. —Henry Ward Beecher

Confession + Forgiveness = Perfection . . . *right?*

Unfortunately, I think we all know it doesn't quite work that way. The question I receive at this point in the discussion goes something like this:

"So, if I continue to mess up and the people I've forgiven continue to mess up, how can we live with a clean slate?"

◄Read Romans 7:14–20. What does Paul do? What is he unable to do? Why is he unable to do it?

Paul is a believer. He's forgiven. He's a mighty servant of God, yet he sins. He wants to do what is right, but he often cannot. He doesn't want to do wrong, but often cannot stop himself.

◄Continue on by reading Romans 7:21–25.

No matter how committed you are to a clean slate, your enemy, the devil, wants nothing more than to sabotage forgiveness, trust, and peace. He is the antithesis of the love you feel for each other and will stop at nothing to erode it.

There are three steps to combat the devil's attacks.

◄Read James 4:6–8.

Step One: _____ the devil.

What does that mean to you?

What are some ways to do that as it relates to the subject of this book?

◄Read Luke 6:27 and Acts 7:54–60.

Step Two: _____ your enemies. _____ for those who have mistreated you.

What does that mean to you?

Clean Slate

What are some ways to do that as it relates to the issues you've been addressing with the Strategic Scenarios?

◀ Reread James 4:6–8.

Step Three: _____ _____ to God and He will _____ _____ to you.

What does that mean to you?

What are some ways to do that as it relates to the hot-button issues you've been addressing?

Immerse yourself in Scripture and prayer to counter the devil's attacks.

Romans 7 (that we looked at above) ends with a description of the battle between Paul's sin nature and his commitment to God. Good ol' Paul admits that he messes up all the time. But we know that, even though he claimed to be at war with the flesh and struggling with sin, he found favor with God. Let's take a look at Romans 8:1–4 to see the resolution:

> Therefore, **there is now no condemnation** for those who are in Christ Jesus, because through Christ Jesus the law of the Spirit who gives life has **set you free from the law of sin** and death. For what the law was powerless to do because it was weakened by the flesh, God did by **sending his own Son in the likeness of sinful flesh** to be a sin offering. And so he condemned sin in the flesh, in order that the righteous requirement of the law might be fully met in us, who do not live according to the flesh but according to the Spirit.

We have a clean slate before God. It's His promise to us in response to the work of His Son, Jesus. With the slate wiped clean for us, we are able to do the same for others. We're all a work in progress; not a single one of us is perfected and complete. We're complete in Jesus—because of Him—but not because of anything we've done. So allow others the same grace of being "in progress" that your heavenly Father is showing you by keeping your slate free from judgment.

> Being confident of this, that he who **began a good work in you** will carry it on to completion **until the day of Christ Jesus**. (Phil. 1:6)

◀ We looked at Philippians 1:6 back in chapter 1, but let's break it down again. Describe what the phrases in the verse mean to you.

Being confident of this
That He who began
A good work in you
Will carry it on to completion
Until the day of Christ Jesus

◀ How can you apply those truths to yourself and your clean slate before God?

◀ How about others and their slate before you? Is it clean in your eyes? Can you forgive an imperfect person?

From that verse, we're reminded that no one is perfect—we're all a work in progress. Commit to forgiving the failures of others, since you know that you will fail and others will forgive you.

The best way to preempt disappointment is to communicate needs and expectations. Each of you, take a moment to share three needs you have regarding the hot-button issues you've been addressing. For example: "More understanding and space when I'm in a bad mood." I recommend you put this list in writing so there's no confusion later.

Parent Commitments

Speak these commitments out loud to your teen(s):

- ◖ I commit to do my best to be a godly example.
- ◖ I commit to having an open mind and heart, ready to listen whenever you need to talk.
- ◖ I commit to being humble enough to admit when I'm wrong, but strong enough to enforce the boundaries I believe are necessary.
- ◖ I commit to _____.
  [fill in the blank based on the needs communicated above]
- ◖ I commit to _____.
  [fill in the blank based on the needs communicated above]
- ◖ I commit to _____.
  [fill in the blank based on the needs communicated above]

Sign: _____

Date: _____

Teen Commitments

Speak these commitments out loud to your parent(s):

- ◀ I commit to do my best to follow your example and do what's right, including being honest at all times.

- ◀ I commit to having an open mind to try to understand that what you ask and expect of me is for my own good.

- ◀ I commit to being humble enough to admit when I'm wrong and honest about how I feel.

- ◀ I commit to _____.
  [fill in the blank based on the needs communicated above]

- ◀ I commit to _____.
  [fill in the blank based on the needs communicated above]

- ◀ I commit to _____.
  [fill in the blank based on the needs communicated above]

Sign: _____

Date: _____

Remember that your enemy, the devil, seeks to sabotage forgiveness, trust, and peace. It's so easy to stumble down a slippery slope.

The pattern of confession, forgiveness, and a clean slate is perfectly portrayed in the relationship you have with your heavenly Father. He loves you, and wants you to walk in complete forgiveness, confident in His love for you. He also wants you to experience that love in your family.

People fail—they've failed you before, and they'll fail you again. You can't wait for God to perfect those you love, but you can allow His perfect love to cover a multitude of sins—grace from Him to you, and through you to them.

> May God himself, **the God of peace**, sanctify you through and through. May your whole spirit, soul and body **be kept blameless** at the coming of our Lord Jesus Christ. The one who calls you is faithful, and **he will do it**. (1 Thess. 5:23–24)

My Prayer for You

Heavenly Father, I lift this family up to You and thank You for their precious hearts that desire to grow closer together. Please guide them as they join hands and walk together in a united purpose to serve You throughout their lives. Facing these Hot Buttons involves release and trust. Help Mom and Dad to use wisdom in knowing when and how to begin the process of that kind of release, and help the teens to respect the boundaries set by the parents and by Your Word. Give them wisdom and strength when it comes to the choices they must make in life. Grant them Your holy sight to see down the road when the way is unclear to them. Help them also to trust each other with some of the tough decisions. As the years go by, remind them of the things they talked about in this book and the commitments they've made to each other. Give them joy as they embark on life with a clean slate. Amen.

Parent's Prayer

Father, I thank You for my family—they're perfect in Your eyes. Help me to take joy in them each and every day—just like You do. You've given us the gift of a clean slate in Your eyes . . . help us to walk in that freedom with each other too. Help me love my family like You do—unconditionally and unselfishly. Please give me wisdom and patience as I help my teens wade through these years. Amen.

Teen's Prayer

Dear Jesus, thank You for forgiveness and for a clean slate. Thank You for a family who wants to serve You and will work hard to make sure I'm on the right path. Please give me wisdom in all things, especially the choices I have to make about these hot-button issues. Help me to do the right thing and to have the strength to stand up to the pressures of life. Amen.

Recommended
Resources

National Suicide Prevention Lifeline: 1-800-273-TALK (8255)
Helplines for kids: 1-800-4CHILD and 1-800-273-talk

Websites

www.choose-NOW.com. The Internet home of Nicole O'Dell and Choose NOW Ministries, dedicated to battling peer pressure by tackling the tough issues and bridging the gap in parent-teen communication.

www.focusonthefamily.com/parenting/schooling/bullying. Focus on the Family is a great family-friendly resource that offers something for every phase of parenting and development, including bullying.

www.hotbuttonsite.com. The Internet home of the Hot Buttons column, where Nicole O'Dell regularly brings you new Hot Buttons scenarios free of charge, for you to use to foster healthy, proactive communication in your family.

www.ncpc.org. The National Crime Prevention Council offers cyber-bullying and Internet safety information for parents.

www.stopbullyingnow.com. What you can do to stop bullying.

www.stopcyberbullying.org. What you can do to stop cyberbullying.
www.theprotectors.org. Training for bystanders.
www.wiredsafety.com. What to do if you are cyberbullied and resources for
    parents.

Notes

1. *Merriam-Webster Online Dictionary.* s.v. "bully," accessed January 25, 2013, http://www.merriam-webster.com/dictionary/bully.
2. Quoted in Robert Faris and Diane Felmlee, "Status Struggles: Network Centrality and Gender Segregation in Same- and Cross-Gender Aggression," *American Sociological Review* 76, no. 1 (February 2011): 48, doi: 10.1177/0003122410396196.
3. Linda Carroll, "1 in 6 Students Is Regularly Bullied, Survey Shows," Children's Health on NBCNEWS.com, October 20, 2010, www.nbcnews.com/id/39758956/ns/health-childrens_health/t/students-regularly-bullied-survey-shows/#.USJPyY6cARk.
4. "Bullying Definition," stopbullying.gov, U.S. Department of Health & Human Services, accessed January 25, 2013, http://www.stopbullying.gov/what-is-bullying/definition/index.html.
5. Stephen T. Russell and Kara Joyner, "Adolescent Sexual Orientation and Suicide Risk: Evidence from a National Study," *American Journal of Public Health* 91, no. 8 (August 2001), http://www.ncbi.nlm.nih.gov/pmc/articles/PMC1446760/.
6. Ibid., citing a 1995 *Developmental Psychology* article.

7. Betsy Rubiner, "Combating Popular Kids and Their Cliques," *Better Homes and Gardens*, March 2004, http://www.bhg.com/health-family /school/back-to-school/combating-popular-kids-and-their-cliques.

8. Faris and Felmlee, "Status Struggles," 67.

9. "Teens and Cyberbullying." Executive Summary of a Report on Research conducted for National Crime Prevention Council, February 28, 2007, http://www.ncpc.org/resources/files/pdf/bullying/Teens%20and%20 Cyberbullying%20Research%20Study.pdf

10. Ibid.

11. Janis Whitlock, John Eckenrode, and Daniel Silverman, "Self-injurious Behaviors in a College Population," *Pediatrics* 117, no. 6 (June 1, 2006), doi: 10.1542/peds.2005-2543.

12. Helen Fisher, Terrie Moffitt, et al. "Bullying Victimisation and Risk of Self Harm in Early Adolescence: Longitudinal Cohort Study," *BMJ* 344 (April 26, 2012), doi: http://dx.doi.org/10.1136/bmj.e2683.

13. Whitlock, Eckenrode, and Silverman, "Self-injurious Behaviors."

14. Ibid.

15. Jill Fleury Devoe and Lynn Baur, *Student Victimization in U.S. Schools: Results from the 2009 School Crime Supplement to the National Crime Victimization Survey* (NCS 2012-314). U.S. Department of Education, National Center for Education Statistics (Washington, DC: U.S. Government Printing Office, November 2011), http://nces.ed.gov/pubs 2012/2012314.pdf.

16. Carroll, "1 in 6 Students Is Regularly Bullied."

17. Ibid.

18. Fisher, Moffitt, et al. "Bullying Victimisation."

About the
Author

Youth culture expert **Nicole O'Dell** resides in Paxton, Illinois, with her husband and six children—the youngest of which are preschool triplets. She is the founder of Choose NOW Ministries, dedicated to battling peer pressure and guiding teens through tough issues while helping parents encourage good decisions, and the host of *Choose NOW Radio: Parent Talk* and *Teen Talk*, where "It's all about choices!" A recent addition to the ministry, Choose HER, focuses on mother-daughter relationships.

A full-time author of both fiction and nonfiction, Nicole's desire is to bridge the gap between parents and teens. Her popular Scenarios for Girls series, the natural segue into the Hot Buttons series, asks teen readers to make tough choices for the main characters and offers alternate endings based on the individual reader's choices.

For more information on Nicole's books or to schedule her for a speaking event or interview, visit www.nicoleodell.com. Follow @Hot_Buttons on Twitter, and like www.facebook.com/HotButtons. Podcasts of *Choose NOW Radio* are available at www.chooseNOWradio.com.